TRIAL *by* MOB

LAST EDITION

THE DULU

VOLUME XXXVIII—NO. 88

THREE NEGROES

POLICE FORBIDDEN TO USE THEIR FIREARMS TO WITHHOLD RIOTERS

Several Officers Injured by Bricks and Other Missiles Thrown by Mob.

Force Totally Inadequate to Handle Situation, Says Murnian.

Believes Order Not to Use Arms Saved Many From Injury.

IMPROMPTU GALLOWS WHERE THREE NEGROES LIVES ARE CHOKED OUT

SOME RESULTS OF ASS
BY FRENZIED M
TUESDAY

INFURIA

H HERALD

26 PAGES

YNCHED IN DULUT

POLICE HEADQUARTERS
LYNCHED THREE NEGROES
TERIOR OF BUILDING IS WRECK

MOB TAKES THREE
M POLICE STATION

GRAND JURY IS CAL
TO FIX RESPONSIBI
FOR HANGING OF

NEGROES ATTEMPTED
ASSAULT WHILE SHOW
WAS AT SOUTH BEND

TROOPS SENT
TO DULUTH BY
THE GOVERNOR

Acts in Response to Telegraphic Request by Sheriff Magie.

Two Companies Arrive at 8 A. M. From Fort Snelling Camp.

A Letter From The Mayor of Duluth, MN June 15, 1993

To remember unpleasant events is painful;
but sometimes an event is so significant
that we must look back in order to move ahead.
Such is the case with the June 15, 1920
lynching of three black circus workers in Duluth.
Though we may wish to forget this painful part of our legacy,
we must not. We must acknowledge the event,
understand how and why it happened, and learn from it.
More than seventy years after that horrendous June day,
racism continues to haunt us.
Those who are its target still feel its sting;
those who are its perpetrators often go unpunished;
and all of us are diminished because of it.
To read *Trial by Mob* is one way of confronting our history
and accepting the book's implicit challenge: to change.
Perhaps James Baldwin said it best:
"Not everything that is faced can be changed;
but nothing can be changed until it is faced."

Gary L. Doty

Gary L. Doty, Mayor

TRIAL *by* MOB

MICHAEL FEDO

A Norshor Book

A Norshor Book

Published by

Theatre in the State, Incorporated

211 East Superior Street

Duluth, Minnesota 55802

Book design by Jerry Hallberg

Project supervised by Harlin Quist

Photograph of lynching provided by

Minnesota Historical Society.

Newspaper photographs courtesy of

The Duluth News Tribune.

Manufactured in the United States of America

by Versa Press, Incorporated

Library of Congress Catalog Card Number 93-60693

ISBN 0-9637394-0-9

DEDICATED

to my mother

Ramona Fedo

(1914-1977)

who first told

me about this

incident

AUTHOR'S NOTES

During the first quarter of the twentieth century, lynch law was a common event in the United States. In 1920, sixty-five persons were lynched. Of these, fifty-seven were black men; one was a black woman.

The incident drawing the most notoriety that year occurred June 15 when a mob estimated at between five thousand and ten thousand persons stormed the jail in Duluth, Minnesota, and lynched three blacks accused of raping a white girl. This is the story of that tragedy.

The characters in this book are real people, and the events and incidents in which they were involved actually happened.

While most of the dialogue used here is exactly what was spoken, there are a few instances where, for the purpose of continuity and smoother reading, or where the exact words were not recorded or remembered, dialogue has been created from documented indirect quotations. In these instances, however, every effort has been made to accomplish this in a manner entirely in character with the persons concerned.

Sources upon which this book is based are numerous. Because this subject still evokes intense feelings among many Duluthians, I have agreed not to publish names of certain persons interviewed during the preparation of the manuscript.

Among those consulted who asked for anonymity were a member of the Max Mason jury, a retired Duluth patrolman on duty during the riot, a man acquitted of rioting charges, a witness at the Leonard Hedman trial, the son of a local judge, the daughter-in-law of a grand jury member, a Duluth attorney whose father was contacted by Hedman's defense, and dozens of eyewitnesses to the lynchings.

Also interviewed for this book were Howard Loraas, a retired police officer who was acquainted with many of the officers on duty during the riot; Dr. Maude Lindquist, professor of history emeritus at the University of Minnesota, Duluth, who knew both Bobby Walsh and Sandra Teale; Veronica Olson, daughter of Sgt. Oscar Olson; the Rev. Joseph Cashen, who provided biographical information about both the Rev. William Powers and the Rev. P.J. Maloney, who tried to prevent the mob from taking the prisoners; William Maupins, Jr., a former president of the Duluth NAACP; Wallace Rodney, Franklin Cox, and Eddie Nichols. There were many others who talked with me, but they merely corroborated evidence, or their information was not substantial enough for inclusion within this book.

The names Sandra Teale and Robert Walsh are fictitious. Because of the freedom needed to tell the story accurately, and to use certain statements by persons who knew "Sandra Teale" and "Bobby Walsh," it was necessary to create names for these two individuals who first told authorities that a rape had occurred. All other names are factual.

Of special value were the newspapers of the times, most notably *The Duluth Herald* and *Duluth News Tribune*, from June 15, 1920, through December 31 of that year. Nearly every day some mention of the lynchings or arrests and trial reports was found in one or both of those daily papers. The *Minneapolis Journal* and *St. Paul Pioneer Press* from June 16 through June 30, 1920, also provided background information and data that was intentionally or inadvertently omitted from Duluth newspapers. Also consulted and quoted were the *Mankato* (Minnesota) *Free Press*, the *Chicago Tribune* , the *Ely* (Minnesota) *Miner*, *The New York Times*, and *Duluth Ripsaw*.

Carol Jenson's article "Loyalty as a Political Weapon: The 1918 Campaign in Minnesota," published in the summer 1972 issue of *Minnesota History* magazine, provided background information on the Public Safety Commision, as did discussions with Jon Willand, a Minnesota historian and instructor at the North Hennepin Community College.

A pictorial booklet, *Mob Violence*, published in 1920 by the Duluth Publishing Company, is a review of the lynching.

More detailed information is contained in the State of Minnesota Historical Society archives, particularly the files of Gov. J.A.A. Burnquist, in which is found the interview between Detective Morgan and Sandra Teale, as well as other matters pertinent to Morgan's investigation. The governor's files also held interviews and findings of Gen. W.F. Rhinow's investigation, including letters and telegrams from Duluthians, James Weldon Johnson of the NAACP, and others representing black concerns.

The archives are also the source for transcripts of the Max Mason trial, found in the files of the State Supreme Court. Material in the files of the Public Safety Commission also proved useful.

LUTH ONE DAY MONDAY, JUNE 14
AMERICA'S FIRST AND FOREMOST CIRCUS
NOW THE FINEST IN THE WORLD
OHN ROBINSON'S
CIRCUS
3 PENS WILD BEASTS 43
Herds of
ERFORMING ELEPHANTS
DROVES OF CAMELS
$1,000,000.00 BIG FREE STREET
PARADE DAILY AT 11 A.M.
SEE THE BIGG
"BABY" "CONC
THE HIPPOPOTAM
DOORS OPEN AT
PERFORMANCE STAR

TRIAL *by* MOB

Gloom was a perpetual state of mind in Duluth, a city frequently shrouded in gray. Mornings were ushered in by the mournful groans of a foghorn, announcing yet another day of damp chill, possible rain, or, perhaps, a June snow.

But it wasn't weather troubling Police Chief John Murphy on this Sunday afternoon, June 13, 1920. He was upset over his deteriorating relationship with the city's Commissioner of Public Safety, William Murnian. Murphy had picked up rumblings of Murnian's dissatisfaction with the way he, Murphy, was running the department. And now Murian had directed Murphy to report to the showgrounds in West Duluth to confer with the parade manager of the John Robinson Circus. The two were to determine the route the parade would take on its 9 a.m. Monday run through downtown: Murphy viewed Murian's order as harrassment, pure and simple.

This was not an assignment normally forced upon a police chief. There were plenty of sergeants who could easily handle it, but Murnian was insistent. It would be an appropriate public relations gesture, according to the commissioner, but Murphy knew better. It was simply a way of letting him know that Murnian, and perhaps the other commissioners too, wanted him out.

As almost an afterthought, Murnian had called and reminded Murphy that it might be wise if the chief suggested that the circus people kept their "niggers" in line.

The chief knew that there had been trouble over some black employees in the circus. After the Robinson show left its home base in Peru, Indiana, in April, some black workers had been accused of assaulting a white girl. But they had been fired. In a way, Murphy perhaps understood the commissioner's concern—what Duluth didn't need was trouble with blacks. Not that there had been problems in the past, but city officials had sensed the growing undercurrent of animosity among many white citizens. Ever since U.S. Steel, the city's largest employer, began importing black field hands from southern plantations to work at the mill, and thereby quelling strike threats by white workers, an uneasy tension existed—especially in the western sectors of the city, where the mill was located, and where most of the city's blacks resided.

Still, the chief perceived his latest directive as a warning of problems ahead. It had to be thus, for Murnian, while publicly defending the force, had privately come down hard on it after a recent incident that saw Lt. Frank Schulte shoot and kill Eli Vuckidonyich, a suspected liquor smuggler. It didn't matter that Vuckidonyich had tried to run down Schulte with his car; the lieutenant should have used more discretion, Murnian said. The chief felt that Murnian held him personally accountable.

During the past week, rumors had begun filtering back to the chief implying that Vuckidonyich was killed because was he muscling in on a major rum-running operation led by the chief, who was supplying Canadian whiskey to prominent local citizens. (The rumor would later result in a grand jury investigation that would indict the chief on charges of smuggling and bootlegging.)

But harassment or not, the chief had his orders, and he carried them out. At three-thirty that afternoon, Murphy checked out a car from the downtown police headquarters at Second Avenue East and Superior Street, and drove to the Omaha yards in West Duluth, where the crews were unloading circus equipment.

He spent nearly thirty minutes reviewing the parade route with the circus manager, and discovered at the same time that the circus employed about one hundred and twenty blacks as cooks and roustabouts. He received assurances that the blacks were quiet and mannerly, and would pose no problems for Duluth police.

The chief told the manager that perhaps it would be best if circus blacks avoided going downtown or hanging around the West Duluth streets. Murphy emphasized that there was a bunch of toughs around who did not care for blacks.

Though he didn't mention it, Murphy no doubt felt that if a group of blacks came swarming into the city, bitterness toward the slowly expanding black community in Duluth would intensify, especially if the blacks ran into some of the World War I veterans from West Duluth.

Veterans had returned to the city with tales of American black soldiers cavorting with white French women. These charges aroused hostilities among the Duluth whites. Within days after their discharges and return to jobs in Duluth, these veterans found blacks working at the steel plant and in the post office. A few of the more radical white spokesmen agitated openly for running the blacks out of town. Some veterans joined the Ku Klux Klan and participated in cross burnings on the boulevard overlooking the city.

For many of these men, the war had never really ended. There were always battles to be fought, injustices, as they perceived them, to be overcome. And the great war remained constant in their minds.

They were often seen on street corners swapping stories of battles at Château–Thierry or St. Mihiel, and the Meuse-Argonne, where the Third Minnesota Infantry saw action. They still sang "Hinky Dinky Parlay Voo."

By June 1920 some of them talked hopefully of U.S. intervention in the Irish situation, or even the Russion revolution. These were fretful times in the world, and such times called for active, dedicated men. The best they could do now was apply pressure to keep black people from white neighborhoods—an effort that was successful; black families lived in Gary, the westernmost tip of the city.

While there had been no fights, no open confrontations, the quiet on the home front was a restless quiet. What the anxious, bored veterans desired was a return to battle and another crack at heroism and its heady sensations—the hugs and kisses from girls, the tear-stained faces of old men and women gratefully waving small American flags. Since Germany had been defeated, and the jubilation of returning home victorious had faded, the glories of the war moved to the forefront of memory, diminishing its horrors.

For some veterans flushed with battlefield successes, working as teamsters, boilermakers, meter inspectors, railroad brakeman, or short order cooks was rife with ennui. Duluth, after the ribald freedom of Paris, was like a withered old woman.

Duluth held no noble causes for these young men in their late teens or early twenties. Duluth demanded nothing of heroic dimensions; few who had not been overseas, who knew nothing of battle, seemed to remember or care about the sacrifices. The veterans remembered, though, that they left the city as boys and returned as men. Maybe boys could be content here, but a man who has seen Paris, who had spilled blood on the battleground, could not.

Among these men were those itching for a cause.

Chief Murphy was aware of their feelings but believed they

comprised no significant threat. They wanted a better life, he reasoned, and why not? They had fought for one. And if they occasionally got together to blow off steam, even drank a little hootch, Murphy had not, and would not, interfere.

What occurred to the chief, however, was that the young veterans seemed to be the only unified body in the entire city. And while citizens certainly came and went as they pleased in Duluth, the city had become compartmentalized into near ghettos. There was little social mingling outside class or nationality strata—with the exception of the veterans.

Scandinavians predominated in Duluth, and operated farms around the city. Comprising the bulk of the middle working class, they were the only group not adhering to strictly ethnic borders. Few lived in the east end, though.

Duluth was divided by vaguely defined ethnic and economic boundaries that found most southern and eastern European immigrants living in western neighborhoods. This arrangement helped keep the city manageable. It was, perhaps, not without forethought that Duluth police had precincts in both the West End and West Duluth neighborhoods.

Financial status of residents mainly improved with eastward migration. And where there was wealth and station, the police seldom intruded.

The city had been properly sedate, caught up in the industrial boom, largely supported by industrialist Jay Cooke. But when that empire crashed in the 1890s, Duluth lost some vitality and spirit; its young grew disenchanted. Possibly, the U.S. entry into the war gave Duluth's young men a sense of purpose.

By nine on Monday, the early morning chill of thirty-five degrees had warmed to the upper fifties. People began lining the street for the circus parade, disregarding the threat of showers forecast for the day.

From his office, Murphy barely noticed the parade, or the thousands who looked on and cheered the four local bands playing patriotic marches, or the lumbering elephant herds, camels, horses, clowns, and trick riders. He was concerned about traffic moving normally when the parade ended. He hoped complaints of animal deposits would not inundate the department. It would be just like the commissioner, he might have thought, to order police to clean up, arguing that droppings created a public hazard.

Duluthians for whom the parade and circus might have been considered bourgeoise may have contemplated visits to the vaudeville houses. Mademoiselle Vera was starring in *The Girl in the Basket* at the New Grand, while the Orpheum featured a new comedy by Mark Swan entitled *Parlour, Bedroom and Bath.*

Cinema attractions included Betty Kilburn in *Girl of the Sea* at the Strand, and Marion Davies in *The Cinema Murder* at the Zelda.

Throughout Duluth, old country burghers in wool caps and tobacco-stained walrus mustaches continued their mutterings over prohibition. Though the city went dry for the first time three years earlier, national enforcement of the Volstead Act made it more difficult to obtain a brew, even in Superior, Wisconsin, just across the Arrowhead Bridge.

Baseball enthusiasts learned from the morning sports pages that Babe Ruth hit his seventeenth home run, proving he was perhaps worth the $125,000 the Yankees paid the Red Sox for his contract, as well as his whopping $20,000 annual salary.

The run on Tanlac at Duluth drugstores had not abated, and had surpassed Lydia Pinkham's Vegetable Compound as the hypochondriac's delight. Tanlac's healing benefits were praised daily in Duluth papers as the cure-all for influenza, grippe, post-operation malaise, typhoid, and pneumonia.

But the big topic in the city on June 14 was the circus, with two shows playing at the West Duluth grounds. By early afternoon a sizable crowd of mothers had packed children into the Oneota streetcars and assembled to view a matinee performance.

The 7 PM Big Top show played to nearly eighty percent capacity. And hundreds more, not entering the grandstand, enjoyed the many sideshows and amusement tents. They would have chatted about the incredible snake handler, Madame X, or the Nelson family bareback riders, before leaving the grounds in an atmosphere pungent with odors of hot dogs, popcorn, and cigar smoke.

Some of these people paused just before nine that night to watch the striking of the animal tents and the loading of the animals and equipment into special boxcars as the circus prepared to move to Virginia, Minnesota, for two performances on the Iron Range.

Among this crowd were Sandra Teale, a nineteen-year-old stenographer, and Robert Walsh, her eighteen-year-old escort. But after a while they apparently drifted beyond the crowd behind the wagons and tents. They were probably among the few who noticed the gathering around the cook tent of black employees who were lounging or shooting craps.

There, nineteen-year-old Elmer Jackson rolled the hot dice. Joyfully, he spun out sevens and elevens, quickly taking a day's wages from the other workers. Their laughter and profane exhortations to the dice could be faintly heard above the blowing calliopes, if one listened carefully. Apparently no one did. It was, after all, only the circus Negroes whooping it up.

One can only speculate what ran through the minds of the girl and boy that night. There were those who said Sandra was loose; Bobby was reportedly fast. Some would insinuate that indiscreet lust prevailed there in the damp softness of the fields away from the crowds, where no one could see, and the heat of passion would have warded off the nighttime chill.

Yet, others would maintain that the two had started something that could bring them both easy cash. Blacks, they said, would give a week's pay for a white girl. Still others would later insist the two had it in for blacks, and simply wanted to make them pay for their blackness.

The two proceeded beyond the cook tent into the field, about fifty yards away. The blacks must have seen them go, and no doubt followed them. The young couple's excursion behind the tent into the field may have been viewed by black employees as an invasion of privacy. No young whites would encroach black turf unless they were looking for trouble.

But whatever happened there, it was not something Bobby or Sandra would ever openly discuss. It was certain, though, that whatever their plans, something went awry.

TRIAL *by* MOB

Duluth was in 1920, and remains today, a thin ribbon of city stretching along the shores of Lake Superior for twenty-five miles at a northeast slant. Its boundaries creep back from the lake at distances varying from a half mile to barely four miles. Across the St. Louis River bay lies Superior, Wisconsin. Together, the two cities have been called the Twin Ports. Both waterfronts support active trade, although Duluth predominates.

The dominant subculture in Duluth, as in all of Minnesota at the time, was Scandinavian.

Superior Street, the main artery, follows the line of the lake and holds most of the major downtown businesses—hotels, clothiers, banks, and restaurants.

Duluth begins in the weedy, barren shambles that is Gary, a neighborhood initially populated by many of the city's blacks, most of whom had come from southern states in search of employment. A few blacks were native to the area of northern Minnesota, their ancestors having been with early logging and trapping concerns. And by 1920, perhaps three hundred of the city's five hundred black residents lived in Gary.

Slightly east was Morgan Park, a Serbian and Slavic settlement built around the large plant erected by U.S. Steel. For many years, Morgan Park resembled a company town—small frame houses on neat, orderly streets. Though some blacks worked at the plant, they were not allowed to live in Morgan Park, within easy commuting distance to the plant.

To the east, another mile or so, was West Duluth, populated by blue collar families, Italians and Finns; workers from the factories settled into neat, serviceable houses painted white or brown, pale greeen, or gray. Their children attended Denfeld High School, and citizens took great pride in Denfeld's athletic dominance over teams from wealthier Central High.

In the central or east hillside area residents lived in ordinary two–story homes as well as stately mansions built by lumber barons during the 1880s and 1890s. Duluth's east end was populated by the professionals—lawyers, doctors, stock brokers—who dwelt in company with bankers and lumber and mining industrialists.

Both Sandra Teale and Bobby Walsh lived in West Duluth neighborhoods. Sandra's father, Arnold, was a mail carrier, and probably walked the city from one end to the other on various routes during his years with the postal service. Perhaps he was comfortable in the cozy blocks around 48th Avenue West and Sixth Street, where folks in similar economic straits tended to pull together, tended to give a feeling of small-town living. But if there was small-town security, there was also the small-town gossip. And with his postman's ear for housewifely gossip, he no doubt had heard rumors about Bobby Walsh.

Bobby was spoiled, many used to say. The kid had too much money for his own good. He took in $140 a month down at the docks in a day when many family men felt fortunate to earn one hundred dollars. There was some resentment, too, on the part of neighborhood men that Bobby got the good job because his father was superintendent at the grain terminal.

But the rumors that would have most distressed Arnold Teale were the continual references to the boy's drinking. Bobby supposedly bought hootch every chance he got. Further, Mr. Walsh didn't directly disapprove, saying that his kid was a little wild, maybe, but would eventually settle down. And at Denfeld, where teachers were considered stern disciplinarians, Bobby was never in real trouble. Folks wondered why. He smoked cigarettes in open defiance of the school ban, and bragged about his easy relationship with many girls. None of this kept him from playing forward on the basketball team, and some parents were upset because the boy rarely bothered to obey training regulations.

What had to disturb Arnold Teale about all this was that his daughter was infatuated with the young man. He may have felt rather powerless because Sandra was, after all, on her own, earning her own keep. He doubtless felt that as a father he had a responsibility to keep his daughter from trouble, and Bobby Walsh looked like trouble. As the relationship between Bobby and Sandra developed, it probably crossed Arnold's mind that Bobby might be taking advantage of Sandra.

Sandra didn't finish school as Bobby had. Perhaps Arnold thought her naive, unable to see behind Bobby's scheming. Mercifully, the gossips didn't talk about the girl when Arnold was within earshot. But they did talk about her. It may have been guilt by association, but if Bobby was wild, and Sandra was often with him, what conclusions could the gossips draw?

At the Walsh home, Bobby was often a center-stage attraction. Peter, his father, liked to talk about the boy's grit and determination. He was also a handsome boy, muscular and stocky, with a ready and confident smile. When his hair was combed straight back off his forehead, many people thought he resembled the man who modeled Arrow shirts in newspapers and magazines. His father liked to think that Bobby was a "chip off the old block."

But others who knew him from the neighborhood and at school, where Bobby had graduated in June 1920, thought him arrogant, especially regarding women. None of this kept many young girls from finding him appealing, despite, or perhaps because of, his apparent penchant for vandalism and other questionable pranks.

Young people, offspring of immigrant or second generation stock, often resented traditional restrictions and were looking ahead to the bright, happy times. They were eager to get the twenties roaring. Bobby was a bit ahead of his time. He could make them roar already.

About eight on the night of June 14, Sandra Teale boarded a Grand Avenue streetcar traveling east, and got off at the Vernon Street stop. She walked several blocks west toward the circus grounds. As she approached the well-lighted circus area, she saw the entrance arch ringed with electric- and gaslights a few feet from Grand Avenue. On the other side of the arch was a passageway sprinkled with sawdust and lined with sideshow tents and concession stands.

The calliope sounds swelled over the grounds, mingling with the delighted shrieks of youngsters and teenagers on numerous rides. Although it was not quite dark, the fully lighted passageway lent a twinkling to the carefree carnival atmosphere.

Sandra had not gone with Bobby to the circus, possibly to avoid a confrontation with her father. But once there, she met him just inside the archway. He was with a small crowd of laughing teenagers. She joined them, and the group wandered through the exhibits and sideshows until shortly after nine. By then, the couple had separated from their friends, and headed toward the tracks behind the menagerie and cook tents, where about two hundred people were watching the crews pack up.

Perhaps the two were holding hands, touching gently, hip to

hip. Or maybe their relationship was businesslike and formal; with no traces of nervousness, they may have discussed approaching the blacks.

If the two watched the animals being led into cars, then crossed to the field where the circus sounds faded, and located a soft spot of ground, they may have engaged in adolescent fumblings, the damp night air playing over their bodies and then . . . or perhaps a contact was made, a price agreed upon. Payment would be forthcoming—after the merchandise was sampled.

If the couple believed they were alone, possibly the observing blacks from the circus laughed, chirping obscenities. Or it might have been that the blacks refused to pay for their pleasure. But a more plausible explanation was that while beyond the menagerie tents, the two may have been robbed by the blacks, or merely insulted. Embarrassed and angered, the couple moved away, the slow drawls and taunts echoing behind them.

Sandra, perhaps confused more than outraged, took her cue from Bobby. And, walking next to him, she must have felt the tenseness in his body, seen his face glower with fierce fury. Perhaps, as he gathered his thoughts, he supposed they could yell rape. That would surely fix the "niggers." They'd hang for *that*! It's no wonder the guys at the steel plant hated "niggers."

The two walked to Grand Avenue, boarded a streetcar, and rode to 49th Avenue West and Grand. From there they hiked three blocks to the Teale home, where they discussed a possible plan of action. After ten minutes Bobby left, possibly telling Sandra to wait until she heard from him.

Sandra went into the house, where she saw her father seated in the front room, reading the evening paper. He saw her but said nothing. "I'm going up to bed," the girl said.

Her father acknowledged her with a perfunctory grunt and returned to his paper.

Hearing sounds of bedtime preparation in her parents' room, Sandra stopped and looked in. Louise Teale, her mother, was putting up her hair. She noticed her daughter, and the girl stepped inside the room. "Mama, I met Bobby tonight," Sandra said. "We went to the circus."

The weary Mrs. Teale perhaps yawned and smiled weakly. "All right, dear, go to bed now."

Sandra bathed and was in bed by ten minutes after eleven.

Bobby, meanwhile, went home to change clothes before reporting to work at the Duluth Missabe and Northern Ore Docks at midnight. He had been working the midnight to eight shift as a boat spotter, watching the holds in the cargo carriers fill up, then signaling the loader to stop. The hours on the job were sometimes an impediment to his active social life, and occasionally dust blew in his eyes or clogged his nostrils. But these were small sacrifices. The pay was good, and with the money he could afford the small luxuries other young men his age would do without.

He was popular with some of the seamen—a rough, brawling bunch who sometimes invited him to participate in poker games when work was slow, or gave him good Canadian whiskey, and maybe even asked him to find girls for them occasionally. No doubt the boy was flattered by the attention of the older men, and pleased to be accepted by them.

When he arrived this night, there were few seamen around, and Bobby paid little attention to their good-natured bantering. He completed the loading of one boat, and shortly after 1AM told his father, who was night superintendent at the terminal, that Sandra Teale had been raped by circus Negroes. Enraged, Peter Walsh phoned Arnold Teale, then called Chief John Murphy at home.

It was nearly two when the chief was awakened by the call. A strident voice told him to get out to the ore docks immediately. But the chief, believing he was talking to a crank, demanded to know why he should leave his bed.

Walsh gave Murphy his name and position but refused to say why he was calling. He pointedly added that the nature of the call was a serious emergency.

"How many men will I need?" the chief asked.

"Figure that out when you get here," Walsh replied.

The chief dressed quickly, then went down to the station and checked out a car for the drive to the West Duluth docks. There, amid shouting and haranguing, father and son reported the details of an alleged assault on Sandra Teale.

At about ten minutes to ten last night, Bobby reported, he and Sandra were starting for home; when they turned to leave, there were six blacks blocking their way; one slipped behind Bobby and grabbed his arms, while a second black placed a pistol in back of his ear. "Be quiet," he allegedly growled, "or I'll blow your brains out."

At that point, Bobby said he stopped struggling. The weapon, he said, scared him. Then a second black went through his pockets, removed his watch, examined it, but returned it. A third black grabbed Sandra, placing his hand over her mouth, while a fourth man removed her ring. Several men looked at the ring, but gave it back.

Then Bobby told Murphy he was pushed forward while four men dragged Sandra to a clump of bushes near the railroad tracks. "Just keep still," the man with the gun reportedly told Bobby. As Sandra was settled behind some bushes, she fainted, the chief was told, and Bobby was made to watch as the blacks "ravished" her. When she recovered fifteen minutes later, Bobby helped her up, and the man with the pistol pointed a direction away from the circus, and told them to beat it. The couple did as they were told, and young Walsh told Murphy that he went home, came to work, and informed his father of the incident.

The story clearly distressed Murphy. Rape was not a usual crime in Duluth, but he knew it always meant trouble. Inevitably, the family of the victim would attempt revenge, but the man inside the officer couldn't fault that. Making matters worse, he probably felt that six blacks violated a young white girl.

Using Walsh's phone, Murphy called the yardmaster at the Northern Pacific station and ordered the circus train detained. However, he was told the train had left and was heading through the Duluth, Winnipeg and Pacific yards, en route to Virginia, about sixty miles north. Murphy made a second call to the DW&P yards, reaching the yardmaster after a dozen impatient rings. "This is Chief of Police Murphy," he barked. "We have an emergency here, and I want the circus train held until I can get there."

His third call went to the dispatcher at the police station. "Get hold of Fiskett, Schulte, Lading, and Olson," he ordered. "Find ten or twelve others and have them meet me at the Duluth, Winnipeg and Pacific lines in West Duluth right away."

Capt. Anthony Fiskett, a veteran officer, the second highest ranking man on the Duluth force, received a call shortly after three and led the contingent of officers to the rail yards by 4:30 AM.

The chief had already begun jogging down the tracks, shouting to his men to divide up and cover both sides. The beefy officers huffed down the line, trying to stay abreast of their chief, and the urgency of his call. Finally Murphy gasped that a white girl had been raped by circus "niggers," and they'd have to get the guilty men. "There were six of 'em," Murphy called.

Nearly out of breath, Murphy pushed forward, prodding his half-wakened men onward, moving them out where the sparse lights of the train glowed a pale blue and yellow in the predawn dark, over a quarter-mile up the tracks. The great train snaked another half-mile around a bend and nearly out of sight. But at least it was stopped, and the approaching officers could hear its engine hissing as they hurried toward the lead car.

Chief Murphy, Capt. Fiskett, and Lt. Schulte, a hard-bitten veteran of twenty-two years service, located the foreman's car and explained the situation. Six blacks had raped a white girl near the menagerie tent last night, the chief excitedly explained. "I want to talk to every nigger that was idle between about nine and ten o'clock last night," he said.

Officers and foremen started down along the train on both sides, rounding up all blacks on the cars, dragging them back toward the end, where the rest were asleep in the segregated sleeping cars.

Police stormed into the sleeping cars and began jerking drowsy blacks from their racks. "Get out of here, you black sons of bitches!" they snarled, poking nightsticks into the cots of the sleeping men or rudely rolling them to the floor.

Max Mason, a twenty-one-year-old hand from Decatur, Alabama, and at five feet four inches one of the shortest of the blacks employed by the circus, was lifted from his rack and dropped on the floor. "Goddamn you! Get out of here!" roared the cop.

Mason, who had been sleeping heavily, reached for his shoes as a blast of chilled air swept through the open car door. He grunted and mumbled incoherently. An officer grabbed his leg and twisted him back to the floor. "Get over there, you black son of a bitch! And don't you talk back!" Shoeless and without his shirt, Mason was pushed outside and thrown in a line with nearly one hundred and twenty other black workers. And in the cold gray morning his teeth chattered; he looked apprehensively around at his shivering, bewildered mates, some of whom gingerly fingered bruises, or leaned over, retching, the results of nightsticks rammed into unsuspecting bellies.

Officers, angered both by the alleged crime and at having been ordered from their beds, then swung their lanterns close to the blacks. Mason would later remember how he envied them in their blue jackets, and thought perhaps he made a mistake by leaving Alabama, where a body wouldn't freeze half to death in the middle of June.

A uniformed officer paced up and down in front of the line. "There was six of you niggers raped a white girl on the circus grounds last night. We'll have every one of you in jail in ten minutes if we don't find those six. So you boys that know something better start talking."

A foreman and several other officers interrupted him, and they conferred, talking in muted voices. Finally most of the blacks were released and returned to the warmth of their cars, while about forty others were kept in the line. "Only those boys might of been around the menagerie tent at the time," a rangy foreman said. "Just them that worked in the Big Top or waited tables." The foreman returned to his coach, while the blacks were left to shiver in the dawn on a West Duluth hill overlooking the slumbering city.

Peter B. and Robert Walsh were brought out then, and the boy was asked to identify the assailants. Looking up and down the line, walking slowly, pausing to examine black faces, Bobby turned toward Murphy and said, "They look pretty much alike to me. I don't know for sure."

The officer exhorted him to try again, telling Bobby that the charge and the crime are very serious matters, and "it would be terrible to arrest the wrong people." But the young man still could not, or would not, make positive identifications.

Moments later, Sandra and her father were ushered to the scene in a police vehicle, and after determining that the girl was not in shock, she was asked if she might identify her attackers. She appeared hesitant, but calm, as she examined the lineup, but said the faces weren't too clear to her. Nevertheless, she identified five whose general size and physique seemed to resemble those who supposedly attacked her.

Meanwhile, Murphy and Schulte, with a blistering crossfire of questions, continued grilling other blacks. Some of the blacks, puzzled or intimidated, gave incoherent or vague accounts of their whereabouts in an attempt to veil the crap game. A few blacks apparently suspected the game was the reason for their detention, and fearing loss of jobs and wages, wished to avoid any confrontation with the law. But from this interrogation, Murphy held eight more men for arrest.

After placing all thirteen under arrest, Murphy released the circus train, which continued on to Virginia. The blacks were loaded into police cars and driven to the jail at the downtown headquarters.

During the next two hours, Duluth officers and the arrested suspects were engaged in an exhaustive questioning intended to coerce blacks into incriminating testimony. There was no such testimony, and seven of the thirteen were released.

Of the six who remained in custody, Chief Murphy believed that five--Elias Clayton, Elmer Jackson, Nate Green, Loney Williams, and John Thomas—might have been involved in the alleged rape. The sixth man, Isaac McGhie, was being held as a material witness. These six, between the ages of nineteen and twenty-two, had joined the circus in Peru the previous April before the troupe's northern swing.

McGhie was placed in a cell in the boys' division on the station's second floor because there was not enough available cell space in the main floor men's department. The others were locked up just after seven, the morning of June 15.

Chief Murphy, Fiskett, and Schulte remained at headquarters after dismissing other officers called out for the emergency. All three, drained by the session, had misgivings about the case, and weren't sure that all the men who might have been implicated were in jail. They sat in the outer office, a room that might have been described in a detective novel as having that remote, heartless, not quite dirty, not quite clean, not quite human look and smell such rooms always seem to have. There was that sameness of nondescript hues of gray-greens, and washed-out blues on walls and ceilings, accented by sterile, carpetless floors.

Finally, Murphy said that the girl and young Walsh were too shaken to make positive identifications, and some of the stories he'd heard from the blacks didn't quite make sense. Just in case, he ventured, they had better round up some of those they'd questioned again. It was agreed that the three would drive the sixty miles to Virginia later in the morning to make more arrests.

After Schulte and Fiskett had gone, the chief remained in the office another fifteen minutes, contemplating the crime. It was the most deplorable he'd encountered in his long service as a policeman. The thought of the assault revolted him, and his sympathy unquestionably rested with the Teale family. What Murphy found particularly galling was the fact that should the blacks be convicted, as they no doubt would be, they'd receive no more than thirty years in the state penitentiary at Stillwater; the poor girl would have to endure the horror for the rest of her life. Sometimes, it seemed to the troubled chief that justice was not served, even when justice was done.

Like many officers of this time, Murphy felt capital punishment should not have been abolished. Even death itself wasn't stern enough for thugs who violated innocent young girls.

At 8:15 AM on June 15, Dr. David Graham, concluding breakfast at home, received a call from Mrs. Teale. She told him something awful had happened to Sandra last night, and could he please come right away. He asked that she take the girl directly to the hospital, but the woman refused, and insisted that Dr. Graham make a house call.

He arrived at the Teale home shortly after nine and found the family in a state of minor hysteria. No one seemed able or willing to state precisely what had happened, but from their nervous chatter, Dr.

Graham deduced that the girl had been assaulted, and he prepared for an immediate examination.

The doctor was somewhat surprised that the girl apparently felt no pain or tenderness as he conducted both a speculum and digital exam. He found normal conditions present, though the girl seemed highly agitated. Dr. Graham believed Sandra might have been suffering from a slight case of nervous exhaustion. That something had occurred was quite apparent to the doctor, but whatever that something was, Dr. Graham privately concluded that it was probably not rape.

15, 1920.

TOR
RISON

WEST DULUTH GIRL VICTIM OF SIX NEGROES

Attacked on Circus Grounds While Watching Loading of Show.

Pistol at Head Keeps Her Escort From Raising an Outcry.

Three Negroes Under Arrest Confess to Their Part...

TRIAL *by* MOB

In the years prior to World War I, Duluth was a city where race relations had never surfaced in open hostilities. There had been occasional veiled threats when members of the Ku Klux Klan held cross burnings, but few white Duluthians could honestly feel intimidated by local blacks.

But they, along with other Minnesotans and, indeed, many Americans, did feel threatened. The war era provoked a "red scare" that prompted nationwide witch hunts and accusations against any suspected disloyal elements. Millions of Americans believed ugly rumors about an imminent "red revolution" erupting in the United States.

Minnesotans keenly felt the hysteria and hatred toward anything smacking of socialism or radicalism, because their state had experienced both the socialistic arguments of Arthur C. Townley's Nonpartisan League, as well as the right-wing, patriotic haranguing from the notorious Commission of Public Safety.

Townley, a bankrupt North Dakota farmer and political organizer, founded the Nonpartisan League, which gave rise to socialistic leanings among many upper Midwest farmers. The league was often linked to Bolshevism by political and business interests; Minnesota Governor J.A.A. Burnquist accused the league's leadership of being connected with "lawless I.W.W., Red Socialists, and pacifists."

So, in April 1917, when Gov. Burnquist urged the legislature to consider a strong bill against anti-Americanism, the Minnesota Sedition Act was approved a full two months before Congress enacted similar federal legislation. This bill made it illegal to print, publish, circulate, or advocate in public before more than five persons, that men should not enlist in the armed forces, or that citizens should not aid or assist the government in carrying on the war. These forbidden activities extended significantly to the Nonpartisan League.

The legislature also created the Commission for Public Safety on April 16, 1920, which granted broad power to " . . . do all acts and things not-inconsistent with the Constitution or laws of the state of Minnesota, or the U.S., which are necessary and proper for the public safety and for the protection of life and public property or private property."

Though its life was less than two years, there can be little doubt that the commission fostered ideas and philosophies that endured generations beyond the existence of the agency. Created independent of any state department, the commission moved to establish county organizations similar to the state structure to "protect itself against those at home whose behavior tends to weaken the war capacity." Its implied powers were so far-reaching that the seven-man unit was eventually held to be unconstitutional, but its extra-legal authorities went virtually uncontested during its reign. Its chief counsel, Ambrose Tighe, said that its preventive force made it unnecessary to wait for disloyalty to disrupt. Prior restraint, in direct violation of constitutional guarantees, was common. And the state's attorney general, Lyndon Smith, said, "While the courts are ordinarily the law's agent for law enforcement, they are not under the constitution, a necessary factor."

Given this inordinate range of interpreting the law and the Constitution, the agency encouraged citizen reporting of disloyal activities, and moved to have the teaching of German removed from public schools. In one case, the commission removed the elected mayor of the town of New Ulm from office after he had advocated that volunteer soldiers rather than draftees be sent into combat.

But much commission activity centered on squelching the Nonpartisan League. While law enforcement officers looked the other way, or even participated directly in the suppression of free speech, speakers were beaten, tarred and feathered, and otherwise harassed and threatened under the blanket protection of patriotic outbursts which were allowable. Some speakers or organizers of the league were routinely thrashed by some sheriffs who further encouraged citizens to act against these dangerous elements in Minnesota. The notion was prevalent that citizens could act with impunity against what they perceived as socialistic, "Red," or disloyal acts, without fear of official reprisal.

An interesting sidelight to the confrontations between the commission and the league is that the league's supported gubernatorial candidate, Charles A. Lindbergh, Sr., father of the aviator, was banned from speaking in Duluth in 1918.

The intolerance, openly and tacitly approved by the commission, took forms of hatred toward Catholics, Jews, and Negroes.

When the war ended, blacks thought that because of their efforts and sacrifices, they had won their place with full rights in American society. This stirring of independence, however, was feared by white America, in the North and South alike. And whites believed that while Bolshevism was bad, a greater threat might come from blacks getting out of hand.

Lothrop Stoddard, a popular lecturer and writer, stated that dark-skinned races constituted a worse threat to Western civilization than either the Germans or the "Reds." And millions believed him.

It was in this climate, then, a time of economic uncertainty, a time when people were polarized along lines of intense patriotism, or pressing for social reform, a time when racial and religious distrust was on the rise, that volatile clashes were not only possible but inevitable.

And in Duluth, the number of blacks had been increasing, although slowly. Some whites became alarmed at the rising black population, viewing it as a potential problem to be carefully observed in coming years.

On the other hand, many well-to-do whites in the city welcomed the influx of more blacks. Cheap domestic labor was not an easy commodity there, and the grand, large homes and private clubs were in constant need of help, routinely assigned to black workers.

Several dozen Duluth blacks, by 1916, were Haitians who came to the city with status akin to indentured servants. Their passage had been paid by Duluth whites whom they were to serve until this "debt" was paid in full. A servile group, many of whom spoke only pidgin English, they often were not aware of their rights under the law, and thus stayed on at slave wages with patrons for years.

Though blacks native to northern Minnesota were few, they vividly recalled that racial incidents seldom occurred until after the war. Black veterans returning from overseas duty in France found that movie theaters they used to frequent without interference now admitted them only if they sat in the last two rows or the front three.

Among long-time black residents, however, the years prior to the war and the return of the veterans signaled at least mildly uncertain times ahead in relations with the white majority. Much of this uneasiness could be traced to the strike-breaking tactics of U.S. Steel which imported blacks to maintain the hourly wage for all workers at twenty-five cents. Perhaps upward of a hundred southern blacks were recruited by the company from plantations to work at the Duluth mill. It was not a difficult decision for the blacks to leave their homes. The offered wage more than doubled their present ten-cent dole, so they came north with the promise of employment at good pay.

On Tuesday morning, June 15, 1920, Duluthians bringing in their morning *News Tribune* from the porch and settling over breakfast found no mention of the alleged assault on Sandra Teale. On the front page they read a syndicated political column by Ring Lardner, and also learned that because Republican presidential nominee Warren G. Harding had decided not to relinquish his Senate seat until his term expired, Gov. Cox of Ohio could not appoint a Democrat to fill the post.

Tuesday, like Monday, was generally cloudy, and a few sprinkles fell early in the day. But the sky cleared by midafternoon, and Duluthians began experiencing the first summery weather of the season when the thermometer peaked at seventy-six degrees. Even by noon, most residents still hadn't heard that anything out of the ordinary may have happened in town Monday night. But word was out in West Duluth, and reaction to it was predictably hostile.

Meanwhile, Police Chief John Murphy had risen shortly before eleven from a fretful dozing. The crime and subsequent investigation had played heavily on his mind; he could not rest. He must also have been thinking that if the case could be quickly solved, it might buy time and focus attention on his positive achievements. He undoubtedly feared eventual indictment on the rum-running charge, but believed a successful completion of this sordid incident could establish a firm defense; certainly, a good job on so volatile a crime would gain him favor with local citizens. What must have particularly troubled the chief, too, was how Commissioner Murnian was going to react.

Schulte and Fiskett were waiting when Murphy arrived at the police station, and Schulte remarked that he had a car washed especially for the trip. Murphy phoned Virginia police, explaining the happenings of Monday night, stating he felt a few more blacks were involved.

He read the suspects' names, and asked cooperation from Virginia police—"If them niggers see us coming, they'll likely run out, so if your boys could make arrests, we'll hop in a machine and drive right up."

Virginia police, however, turned the matter over to the St. Louis County sheriff's deputies, and three of them arrived at the grounds after the Robinson Big Top had been positioned.

Lt. Schulte was a precise man, and he noted time of departure from the police garage at 12:02 PM. He, too, must have been nervous about the trip. He had, in fact, been agitated over routine business ever since that night of June 2, when he had to kill Eli Vuckidonyich. The press had jumped on him for that, and it was a shame that the incident warranted a grand jury probe.

Schulte was grateful that Murphy hadn't suspended him during this investigation. He knew the chief understood what it was to be a cop under fire—to try and do your job and have everything you do chewed over and spit out by everyone.

Each officer would have preferred taking the more comfortable train up to the range city, but all understood the importance of the task. Besides, the train wouldn't leave until 3:50 PM, and with any luck at all the car could make the sixty miles up the Vermilion Road before then. As the lowest-ranking man of the three, the chore fell on Schulte to be the driver.

Weary from the previous night, conversation among the three was sparse during the first hour. But as the car passed through the village of Twig, about twenty miles north, Fiskett expressed concern about the situation back in Duluth. He said he was disturbed at what might happen with the three ranking officers out of the city, adding that even the mayor was out of town. Mayor C.R. Magney had gone to Bemidji for a conference. "Maybe we should call the office and check on things in town," Fiskett suggested to Murphy. Schulte added he'd been thinking the same thing, but dismissed it—"I mean down south you'd expect trouble. But not up here."

Still, Murphy said he was concerned, and told the others he'd call as soon as they reached Virginia.

Meanwhile, in Virginia, sheriff's deputies approached an impatient circus foreman to explain their presence. They'd have to arrest ten blacks, and they asked the foreman to produce them. The suspects were quickly bound over to the officers who took them back to the small county jail. They anticipated full confessions before Murphy's arrival.

Louis Hays, a properties man in the Big Top, was thrust next to Max Mason at the end of the line. The blacks who faced the deputies clearly resented the new harassment, but kept silent when a young officer stepped toward them and demanded to know who was responsible for the outrage. The officer grinned malevolently, drew his pistol, and pointed it first at Hays, then at Mason. "Talk!" he ordered. "Let's have the whole story."

"Don't know nothing," the squat Mason said slowly.

"You know plenty, all right. If you don't talk, I'll kill you!"

The blacks shuffled nervously, and cast sidelong glances at Mason. The little guy had better watch himself, they thought. Mason shrugged. "Go 'head and shoot, 'cause I don't know nothing, so I can't say nothing."

The deputy slowly cocked the pistol and brought it close to Mason's head. "We'll see about that, *boy*!" he said, holding the barrel at Mason's ear for several seconds. Finally, he retreated, and holstered his weapon.

During the lunch hour on Tuesday, the reported rape had circulated widely throughout West Duluth. Particularly quick to react with anger were the young men from the neighborhood. Many of them were veterans of the war who had witnessed racial strife in the European theater. Some had observed Klan cross burnings but didn't join in, feeling that sort of thing belonged in the South. But after noon, word moved rapidly around the working-class neighborhoods, and the cry rose everywhere that justice must be done. After all, this was one of their own—a West Duluth girl. And the anger, frustration, and rhetoric was not to be lost on the young men returned from war who saw again an opportunity to do something that should ensure protection for helpless women and children.

Louis Dondino was a thirty-eight-year-old widower who operated an auto transfer business in West Duluth. His prize possession was a one-ton green Ford pickup. And because his work centered around cars, he was looked up to by younger men who were becoming fascinated with automobiles.

It was midmorning when he caught the first news of the alleged assault, and he reacted with more anger than others. He had long distrusted blacks, having occasionally observed black boys loitering around the yard, looking at parts and equipment. He'd been hit by petty theft from time to time, and tended to blame the black boys. Still, minor theft was one thing, rape quite another. He may have considered calling his late wife's uncle, Bill Murnian, to see what might be done. But Uncle Bill didn't handle the daily workings of the police department, and probably was busy enough without Louis bothering him.

Dondino never felt the reported rape was a rumor, as did some others. And about midafternoon Dondino got in his truck and started driving around the West Duluth business district, hoping some of the boys he knew down the street might have some idea of what to do. If they didn't, he had plenty of ideas of his own.

Upon high school graduation, Leonard Hedman had been

regarded by many in West Duluth as a young man of ideals, a young man with a fine future ahead of him. Others, however, viewed him as something of a prankster. This opinion was most likely held by those who might have been jealous of the young man's accomplishments at Denfeld High School, where he played football, and was known as the soap box orator of his class. He later served in the army during the war, and was determined to earn a law degree. His present employment as a railroad brakeman was providing him the opportunity to save money for his education.

Among former classmates, he was best remembered for his ringing delivery of the Percy E. Thomas speech, "The American Infamy," during declamation competition with other high schools. This speech had been written by Thomas during his undergraduate years at Northwestern University, and was originally delivered at the Northern Oratorical Contest at the University of Wisconsin in 1900. The speech, which bitterly denounced the lynching of blacks in the South, described the work of a mob in a southern town. It quickly became popular among students in the Duluth high schools. The closing paragraph of that oration declares:

"The majority of both North and South knows that lynching is an evil; but this insight must be heated to action which shall restrain the less thoughtful of the majority. We must have sentiment which guarantees a trial to the accused before a judgment bar uncorrupted by the gangrene of prejudice; we must have a sentiment that visits upon the guilty punishment as swift and unerring as the hands of God; a sentiment that restrains the shirking Sheriff from washing his hands in innocence before the mob: a sentiment that desperately determines to lift the law in its majesty far above the maddened judgment and revengeful spirits of the rabble; a sentiment that will eventually say, 'killing by the mob is murder; the reign of lynch law anarchy; and by the help of God, this American infamy must go'."

But Leonard Hedman was now twenty-three years old and confronted by what seemed a terrible reality—black men had ravished a white girl; at the Steel Plant black men were taking jobs that rightfully belonged to friends of his. He must have wondered where they would go next. Where will insidious encroachment stop? And on that day Hedman, like many others, was troubled that the law would react meekly in view of the horror perpetrated on the young girl.

By late afternoon Hedman apparently wandered the streets of West Duluth, finding the rape uppermost in heated street-corner conversations. The scattered crowds seemed leaderless and frustrated in their impotent rage. They argued about the law that allowed rapists to get off with thirty years instead of death. There was, Hedman must have noted, certain agreement that rapists should die. And if the law wouldn't kill them, then by God, the people would.

John Burr was a twenty-four-year-old shipyard employee supplementing his income by working part-time in a West Duluth pool hall. He hadn't wished for the second job, but with a seven-month-old baby in the house, the added money was necessary.

Though repulsed by the reported crime, Burr held reservations about storming the jail as many at the pool hall were suggesting. He told a number of men wandering in that he wouldn't participate in anything like that. But, privately, he decided he'd go along for the ride—just out of curiosity.

Nate Natelson was not a West Duluthian. He clerked at a Michigan Street clothing store, and probably viewed his job as a stepping stone toward store management and eventual ownership of a retail outlet. He looked to a promising business career in Duluth—a city where he believed Jews had a good chance for success. There were prosperous Jews in Duluth, and many had made considerable contributions to civic betterment. Natelson believed that one day he might even be able to donate funds toward a new hospital or playground.

Jewish migration to Minnesota during the early 1900s concentrated heavily on Minneapolis. It was a more vigorous, more exciting city than many in the Midwest—a city with unlimited economic opportunity. But many Jews felt the sting of anti-Semitic bias in Minneapolis, and found its existence much less significant in Duluth.

Natelson was not unmindful of the Jewish attitude toward Duluth, and he wouldn't have wished to deliberately jeopardize the good fortune many Jews enjoyed there. Yet he was a white man, too, and he felt the same awful revulsion over what supposedly happened to the girl. Further, he knew many young men from West Duluth. They shopped in his store. He knew and understood the attitudes of the Duluth laborer, and empathized with his outrage. These were honest, hardworking people, and Natelson liked them. They had few pretenses, put on no airs. And if they were going to get themselves involved in something up at the jail, well, maybe he'd go along. *Somebody* had to see to it that this horrible incident was never again repeated, he believed. The people would surely decide on that, and Jew or not, Natelson was part of the people.

Albert Johnson was excited. A nineteen-year-old accountant for the Duluth Street Railway, he had heard talk throughout the city about the rape and the rumblings about a group getting together to tear down the jail and take the blacks. And that would be something to watch, he thought.

For thirty-four-old Gilbert Henry Stephenson, a bachelor, day-to-day living had been pretty much routine and dull. Nothing of consequence had happened to him in the dozen years after he left the farm near Des Moines where he was born. One dead-end job had led to another, and during the past eight years, he'd shifted from one town to another, picking up jobs when available, managing brief, unenduring relationships with a number of faceless, nameless women who waited tables in cafes along the way.

He'd toiled as a laborer for contractors, as a carpenter's apprentice, serving the past two years as a truck driver for Bloom and Company in Duluth. At his age, he'd given thought to possibly settling down, but prospects did not appear promising. A temporary position had taken on a bit of permanence, and the wanderer had resigned himself to a restless routine of sameness. Work, then back to the boardinghouse for supper. Maybe a movie on Saturday night.

But this rape case—now, there was something. Stephenson must have been excited as much as angered. There was talk all over town about how a big gang of fellows was going to attack the jail, and *that* would be something.

Twenty-seven-year-old William Rozon had seen his glory days during the war dwindle into frustration and monotony. An unemployed fry cook, he left his previous job because a man who had seen half the world, a man who had fought for his country, was entitled to something better out of life. Rozon spent his recent days roaming the West End streets, looking for a job. He wanted work a man could be proud of, just as he had been proud of his uniform, proud of his service.

This talk about getting together to take "niggers" from the jail stirred him. That would be fine. White men had to stand together; there was no question; keep their women safe. Count on him if anything came up.

And also count on twenty-year-old Carl Miller, a boilermaker's helper . . . and Bill Hughes, a teamster . . . and Pat Olson, a meter inspector . . . and dozens, perhaps hundreds, of others.

Sgt. Olson had been sleeping soundly at 2:45 that morning when the call came from headquarters, telling him to report for duty. Arriving just before 3:30 from his home, he was told a girl had been raped on the circus grounds, and he had joined other officers at the rail yards to question the blacks.

He accompanied the suspects back to the station, where he remained until after they were jailed. At 7:30 he returned home and slept a few hours before his wife called him down to lunch at 2:30. He reported back at headquarters at 3:55 and took command of the station five minutes later.

At the time he assumed command, he asked if anything out of the ordinary had turned up, or if there was something he should know regarding the blacks. He received a negative response. But one officer had dismissed, as a crank, a phone call from a man identified as William Lashells, who told the officer he'd heard rumors about men coming down to take the blacks from the jail. Olson would not learn of this phone call.

William Lashells would show himself to be one of the few

concerned citizens during the most gruesome time of Duluth's history. Not only was he concerned, but he would later suffer for his concern and involvement.

About 2 PM Lashells had stopped into a pool hall on Central Avenue in West Duluth to buy a cigar. Spending an idle moment watching a game of snooker, he heard three young kibitzers discussing the alleged rape. He believed he heard them plan to take the captives from the police and hang them. Lashells lit his cigar and scanned the vendor's newspaper for details of the rape, but found none. Until that moment he believed talk of the rape had been nothing more than rumor. But during the morning hours, and into the afternoon, discussion throughout West Duluth had been angry. Lashells had heard the inevitable talk of revenge, but had dismissed that, too, reasoning that nobody would act on unfounded rumors. As he left the pool hall, he observed groups of men clustered about on the street, talking loudly, gesturing, their faces red with fury. Some were cursing police, saying rapists no longer burn in the electric chair but go to jail for ten or fifteen years, then get out and do the same thing all over again.

Lashells walked back to his home and decided to warn the police. "There's a mob from West Duluth coming down to the station tonight to take the niggers out and kill them," he told an unidentified officer who answered the call.

"Oh, that's all right," Lashells was told. "We're expecting them."

Ninety minutes later, Lashells heard men on Central Avenue talk of buying dynamite to blow up the jail, and he tried persuading them not to carry out the threat because it would take innocent lives as well as guilty.

"What if she was your own flesh and blood?" someone screamed at him. "What would you do? You think black scum like that deserve to live?" Six men got in a nearby car and sped off, shouting that they were going to kill those "niggers."

Lashells wondered if he shouldn't call headquarters again, but decided it was a police matter now, and he'd already done his duty by informing once.

At 3:30 PM Tuesday afternoon, Lt. Frank Schulte parked the Duluth police car in front of the jail in Virginia, pleased that he had made rather good time. He was thinking to himself that after some coffee and a bite to eat, he'd be home by midnight.

But Duluth officers found Virginia deputies irritable and surly, claiming that the blacks refused to talk. Chief Murphy indicated he could break the silent conspiracy, and would do so. Then, remembering Fiskett's earlier warning on the road, he tried to phone Duluth, but a loud buzz in the line made conversation impossible. It was nearly 4:45 before he was able to get through with a decent connection.

Sgt. Olson took the call, and when Murphy asked if things were normal downtown, Olson replied, "There doesn't seem to be anything unusual."

Murphy said he didn't think anybody "would make trouble over the niggers," but added, "Just in case, get every available man where you can reach him on short notice." Olson agreed, but tried to put the chief at ease. "It don't look like trouble right now," he said.

Completing the conversation with Murphy, Olson stepped to the front of the department and looked out on Superior Street. It was orderly, and Olson paid little attention to a larger-than-normal number of people downtown. Even at that, the veteran officer had no reason to doubt that he and his men could handle any situation that might arise. The people of Duluth were decent, and law abiding, he felt, believing that Duluth, whatever its shortcomings, was not Georgia or Alabama.

Oscar Olson's feelings were not unlike those of virtually all Duluth police. The probable raping of a white girl by black men struck them as as horrible an offense as could be committed. He, like the others, felt rage and disgust.

As a private citizen, Oscar Olson might well have decided to thrash the Negroes. He'd have been just the man to do it, too. A shade over six feet two, Olson weighed two hundred and eighty-five pounds. Because of his immense girth, he appeared older than his thirty-two years. But he was amazingly agile; many an unfortunate thief thought he could give the slip to the "fat old man," only to be surprised when Olson overtook him. His reflexes were those of a highly trained professional athlete. And, in fact, Olson had boxed and wrestled professionally.

His sense of rage at the deed and compassion for the Teale family were no doubt heightened by the presence in his own home of two small daughters. Briefly, his mind wandered to how he might have reacted if a similar assault had been made on one of his children.

Olson was familiar with lynch law, having read numerous accounts of its application in the South. He dismissed a gnawing apprehension that it might occur in Duluth, and examined a roster of available officers. About 5 PM he again looked out on Superior Street. Crowds had begun filling the street, and a number of young men were standing across the street, eyeing the station. Olson grew anxious, but told himself that maybe folks came downtown every day in crowds, that he just never paid attention before.

Although Olson had reported that downtown was normal when the chief had called from Virginia, the sergeant was vaguely apprehensive. The tenseness quickened when the phone rang again at 5:05, and an anonymous caller asked if Olson had heard about the attempt to get the blacks.

Now Olson had to act. He sent a motorcycle officer out with instructions to see if he could spot any groups that seemed to have mischief on their minds. The officer was to find out what the groups were discussing, and was told to go into the various pool halls downtown where there might be young men hanging around.

At that same time, near the Arcade Cigar Store on Third Avenue West and Superior Street, Patrolman Bill McKenna, a six-year veteran of the force was walking his beat. He, too, had noticed unusually large numbers of people on the street, and became disturbed. Stopping at the Lyceum Theater taxi stand, he sidled up to a driver and asked what was going on.

"Jeez, Bill, there's talk all over about a whole bunch from West Duluth coming down tonight to get the colored boys," the cabbie said.

"They better not," McKenna replied, moving away. A glance at his watch revealed the time at five past five. It was unthinkable, he reasoned, that anybody from Duluth might try to take prisoners from police. It was just talk. Sure, folks were steamed up, but who wouldn't be? He caught snatches of angry conversation as he continued on his beat, and had the feeling that more people than usual seemed to be staring at him. Well, he'd be back at the station by seven. He could tell Oscar about what he'd seen and heard then.

At 5:15 PM Olson's emissary returned to the station, reporting that while many folks were on the street "sort of like the week before Christmas" he could find no information about any abnormal activities.

Olson was skeptical. A plainclothesman would have been better for the job. One of the detectives. Folks naturally clammed up when they saw the uniform. Glancing out the window again, Olson must have felt a momentary clutch of fear. There were simply too many people milling about. And for the first time, he worried about the ability of his men to cope with an unseemly situation. Had their training enabled them to handle mobs? He must have thought about his own rookie days, when there was no prior training at all. He might have remembered the standard advice given all newcomers on their first day of duty. "When you work the bowery," some old hand would say, "and you find a drunk, just give him a good kick in the ass and tell him to go to his room."

But even in 1920, police received no firearms instruction, and certainly no lessons in mob control. Police in 1920 were selected for brawn, not brains. They were scrappers and could handle themselves in a fight. They'd be all right, Olson reckoned—if they didn't panic.

Apprehensive, Olson did not go out for supper, and was still at his desk when a West Duluth businessman came in and said he heard there might be an attempt to lynch the blacks later that night. Olson responded that the police had heard some rumors, but assured the man that police were ready. He noted the time as just past 5:40.

In another part of the city about that time, a number of young men boarded Louis Dondino's truck and started to drive through the West Duluth streets. Many appeared grim and determined, but others were laughing and joking. As the truck moved slowly through the neighborhoods, men on board shouted, "Come on! Show what kind of men you are! The niggers raped that girl, and she might be dead! . . . What if she was your sister or daughter? . . . Join the necktie party!"

Men in the truck held lengths of rope over their heads. One young man fashioned a noose and wrapped it around his throat, then affected an exaggerated choking and gagging pantomime. The men had tied a long piece of rope to the back of the truck and from the streets and sidewalks other men grabbed onto it and marched behind, encouraging others to join.

The procession grew rapidly. Young men barely out of high school were urging older men to come with them. "What if the girl had been your wife or daughter?" they hollered. Again and again.

"And they was *niggers* besides!"

A number of observers, however, did not take the parade seriously. "Go south!" a few hecklers taunted.

"Not till the blacks snakes are hung."

A few older men took up with the youths, tagging along behind cars and trucks. Occasionally, an older man swung up onto Dondino's truck, and received lusty cheers.

The parade steadily swelled as it swept slowly eastward, reaching Fourth Avenue West and Superior Street by 6 PM. Hundreds of Duluthians waiting for streetcars saw the white men making threats against the black prisoners. Then Dondino's truck passed the police station, where a dozen men jumped out. The truck circled back to Eighth Avenue West, and the procession started another drive through downtown.

Shortly before 6 PM, five young men had entered Siegel's Hardware Store across the street from the police station. The clerk, in the process of checking out for the day, did not immediately observe them as they looked around, their eyes intent, their movements purposeful.

Finally, the clerk noticed them, and started from behind the counter, asking if he could help. The men didn't answer until one finally hollered from a rear corner. "Here." The others hurried back and began stripping yards of rope from a large wooden bail. The clerk assisted in moving the bail. "This is on the house, boys," he said. "You're doing a good thing."

UTH HERAL

EVENING, JUNE 15, 1920.

FAMOUS POLICE INSPECTOR OF N. Y. SENTENCED TO PRISON

DOMINICK HENRY.

WEST DULUTH GIRL VICTIM OF SIX NEGROES

Attacked on Circus Grounds While Watching Loading of Show.

Pistol at Head Keeps Her Escort From Raising an Outcry.

Three Negroes Under Arrest Confess to Their Part in Crime.

CHOICE CONVE BY

UNDER-SECRETARY WHO SUCCEEDS FR

NORMAN

L SUPPORT K WORKERS

L. Pledges Aid to kers on Atlantic Coast.

First Step Against n Shop" Policy of nship Interests.

DIVORCED

TRIAL *by* MOB

Early editions of the evening paper, *The Duluth Herald*, began carrying the story of the alleged assault, running a front-page headline—WEST DULUTH GIRL VICTIM OF NEGROES. It was not the lead story, however, covering just one column and recounting the incident in about two hundred and fifty words, much as it had been given to investigating officers earlier that morning.

Twenty-year-old Eddie Nichols, a black truck driver, had not heard of the assault by 6 PM, when he finished work. He stopped to visit his brother, William, in West Duluth. The young man entered the house after a perfunctory knock, and found the home strangely silent. On the living room sofa, Nichols noticed the headline and froze.

A World War I veteran, he remembered that the most tense and heated combat he's seen during eighteen months abroad was the rioting between white and black American troops in Bordeaux, over whether a black soldier could be convicted of rape for cavorting with a white French prostitute. On the verge of panic, Nichols knew whenever black men were sexually involved with white women, deep trouble inevitably followed. He also recalled that a black soldier in his company, carrying on a lengthy affair with a French girl, had been convicted in military court of raping her, and executed.

"There's going to be a lynching." Nichols said hoarsely as his brother entered the room. "There's going to be a lynching."

William's family, already shaken by the headline, tried to remain calm. "It's Duluth, up *north*," they argued without conviction. "Maybe things will just blow over."

Eddie was going to stay for supper, but he was no longer hungry. He left William's house and headed home, boarding a streetcar on Grand Avenue. As the car passed through volatile neighborhoods, Nichols saw men shouting and shaking their fists. He was more aware of being watched, and his horror and fright did not diminish when twice he saw whites salute clenched fists at him and holler, "We're gonna get *all* the niggers in town."

Nichols observed the mob forming on Third Avenue West. He tried to keep his gaze straight ahead, hoping, praying, there would be no incident on the streetcar. He rode safely through downtown and on up the hill. White people seemed to be looking at him, and, in his fear, he regarded their impassiveness as hostility and hatred.

He left the streetcar at Sixth Avenue East and Sixth Street, walking one block east to his residence. The quiet of the neighborhood seemed grossly unreal, removed from the vengeance-prone mobs on Superior Street, barely a mile away.

If he hadn't seen the mob, if he hadn't seen the paper, Eddie Nichols might have thought this a pleasant June evening, fine for a movie date with his girlfriend. A warm breeze gently lifted the peonies in front of the house at 619 North Fifth Avenue East, where Nichols boarded with the family of Wallace Rodney, a twenty-six-year-old shipping clerk. Rodney's fears had turned to outrage and frustration as he, too, had heard that all blacks would be killed.

Though a few black families lived in the hillside neighborhood, most were still in Gary, where the semblance of community could offer modest security. But blacks scattered about the rest of the city were isolated, cut off from those who might lend badly needed moral support.

Nichols rushed inside the house and went to his room, where he got a .45 automatic pistol he had purchased from army surplus. He loaded it, and came back into the front room. "We're going to be all right," he said huskily, though his hand trembled as he clutched the weapon. "Nobody's going to take us."

Quickly, he locked all the doors in the house, then sat in the front room, his eyes glued on the front door, his hand sweating around the heavy pistol.

Another hillside black, William Maupins, Sr., finished work at 6 PM, and walked along Superior Street toward his streetcar stop when he spotted a mob forming. He inquired about what was happening, and a white man sneered, "They're going to lynch some niggers."

Maupins didn't wait for the streetcar, but bolted up the hill to his home at Fifth Avenue East and Sixth Street, barricading his family inside. A rational man, Maupins started calling other black families in Duluth, offering advice and encouragement when he could. Duluth blacks were resolute and determined; they would fight if they had to.

Also at about six that night, William Murnian left his upstairs office at police headquarters. He, too, noticed the unusually large gathering downtown, but assumed the police could handle any disturbance. It simply wasn't his affair.

Elected to his post in April the previous year, Murnian had seen police operations run smoothly until the past few months. Given the slightest reason, he planned to dismiss Murphy and get the department on its feet again. This would divert attention from the negative aspects of the department, and enable him to appear to be a forceful man making major decisions.

Murnian was well liked as a politician, and was considered a friend to the workingman. As commissioner, however, his role with the police department concerned policies and theories. He did not deal with day-to-day operations.

As one of four elected commissioners who governed the city with the mayor, Murnian had been appointed to oversee public safety. And, presently, his policies dealt with traffic, now that Duluthians were beginning to use autos. Most criminal procedures remained in the hands of the chief.

But as Murnian stepped into the street, he paused to survey the crowds. A public official, he was recognized by some who greeted him as he continued his walk home for dinner. He was free for the evening, and contemplated turning in early.

At seven Sgt. Olson instructed the switchboard operator to call all off-duty men and have them report for immediate duty.

No question now. Something was up. When Olson had taken a brief stroll a hundred yards west of the station, the men grew silent and stared at him. Most of these people were law-abiding citizens, and it was this fact that had scared Olson.

Other officers inside the station were looking to Olson for assurance and instructions. "We'll be all right," he called out, sensing their anxiety. "Let's not lose our heads. That's the main thing."

Sweat trickled down his cheek and welled in the dimple on his chin. Suddenly, he placed a call to Sheriff Frank Magie at the St. Louis County jail. Magie wasn't there, but Olson left word with the jailer to notify Magie that extra men might be needed downtown if the situation worsened. Then Olson called the fire department and requested standby assistance. Hoses and men might be needed.

Throughout the past hour there had been talk about the green truck loaded with young men moving back and forth along Superior Street. At one point the procession led by the truck had created a minor traffic jam near Eighth Avenue West and Superior Street, which was unsnarled by Duluth policemen. Despite the threats from truck riders—"Let's hang the black niggers," and "Join the necktie party"—the officers apparently did not think the young men meant to carry anything further than to make a protest at city hall. Oscar Olson was not advised of this activity until just before 7:30 PM, when a sergeant from the West End called and asked if Olson had seen the truck. Olson said he had not.

"Well, there's a bunch of young fellows on it, and things don't look so good," the other sergeant said.

"Why didn't you stop it?" Olson asked, his agitation heightening.

"I would of, but I didn't see it until after it went by, Oscar. Probably she'll be near downtown by now."

Olson groaned. "Well, get your men, and get down here right away!" He slammed down the receiver, then picked it up and called Murnian at his home.

A prominent local attorney, Hugh McClearn, had noticed the commotion on the streets throughout the afternoon from his downtown office. He knew why the mobs were gathering. Aware that the mayor and the three top police officials were out of town, McClearn feared potential disaster.

About seven that evening McClearn went to the Commercial Club and notified District Judges William Cant and Bert Fesler of mob activity that seemed to be intensifying along Superior Street. Both judges left the club with McClearn and hurried to the station, arriving as a barrage of bricks was hurled at headquarters. At this point, the mob had not begun to rush the station, though most front windows in the department had been smashed.

Judge Cant, a forceful if not self-righteous man used to being paid homage from his long years on the bench, made his way to the front of the station. Instantly recognized, the mob quieted as he held up his hands for silence. "Men, I can understand your anger tonight," he began, sizing up the mob and hedging for time.

"Damn right!" someone shouted back. That reply was accentuated by others in the mob, and the judge waited until the crowd settled before continuing. "This is wrong. Look what happened in Omaha. The riot there disgraced that city. The honor of Duluth is at stake. Most of you are law-abiding citizens, and if you do this terrible thing, you will never live it down, and neither will Duluth." Cant, a sober man of frequently eloquent rhetoric, found the mob in no mood for his preaching.

"Hell, Judge," one man hooted, "You'd only have to hang 'em yourself anyways. We'll save you the bother."

Judge Fesler, noting the apparent futility of Cant's persuasion, did not speak to the mob, but instead talked to individuals within the mob and asked their help in dispersing the crowd. Fesler, a widely respected judge, might have had more rapport with the men in the mob. He was a jurist with a layman's sense of humor. Humor was not out of place in his courtroom. But his efforts possibly added fuel to the mob's arsenal, for he said that the police were dreadfully undermanned, and that they needed help. He tried persuading men in the mob to assist the police in controlling the crowd, and to help protect the lives of the prisoners.

Few responded positively, though a number did undertake halfhearted attempts to talk others into letting the law run its course. But Fesler believed that most of the mob hoped the lynching would take place. They had come downtown for some action.

Yet the talks by Cant and a few unidentified men had a temporary effect in disorganizing the mob, leaving it leaderless. Men still milled about, waving tools and ropes, but they fell back, away from the front of the station, and Olson and his men assumed what appeared to be a solid defense posture in front of the station.

Cant and Fesler, believing they had quieted the potentially explosive situation, left the scene and phoned Virginia, attempting to locate Murphy. Cant thought that perhaps cooler heads would prevail, and that law-and-order advocates had taken some initiative from the mob. In truth, the judges had been almost impressed with the orderly attitude of the crowd. Surely a group of that size—almost politely listening to Judge Cant—was not bent on destruction and violence.

Their opinion had not been shared by Fred W. Beecher, a thirty-three-year-old executive with the Peyton Paper Company located on Second Avenue West and Michigan Street, about five blocks from the police station. A major in the Minnesota National Guard, Beecher had been trained in mob control while on stateside duty during the war. He first became aware of the mob activity in the late afternoon, and as his secretary was leaving for the day, he told her to be careful. "It looks like there might be an attempt at lynching over there," he said.

He remained at his desk until 7:45 PM when he went for dinner at the Congress Cafe, six blocks from the station. He was concerned about the situation developing at police headquarters, and even from inside the restaurant could hear the howling down the street. He thought that his military training in quelling riots might be of some value to local police, but he wasn't known to them, having moved to Duluth from Minneapolis only two months earlier. He thought, too, that police should be able to handle things, and if big trouble really unfolded, the local militia would be summoned to end the disturbance.

However, the gnawing uncertainty existed, and Beecher was unable to eat his dinner. He went outside; a short walk among the mob convinced him that the people were not about to go overboard. His mind eased slightly, and he returned to his office.

Inside the jail, the black prisoners were acutely aware of the turbulence on Superior Street. They'd seen the Klan in action back in their southern homes, and those night riders and cross burners were among contributing factors to their desire to migrate northward. Life would be better for a black up north, the men no doubt reasoned. But none of the inmates in the Duluth jail had ever confronted intense white violence before. And their fear at that moment was compounded by confusion. They were, after all, in a northern city, where so-called racial hatred was nonexistent.

There were reports that during initial outbursts and rioting, the prisoners exhibited little overt anxiety, believing that Duluth police would certainly subdue any ugly eventuality. They told themselves that the sheriff here wasn't a Klan member; that police had guns and would use them.

At 7:45 PM no lights were on in the homes of Duluth blacks. Children were hustled off to early bed, while adults gathered in living rooms, talking in hushed, nervous whispers. Occasionally somebody mumbled a prayer. No one thought of dinner or sleep.

The Duluth city jail was situated in the rear of the police station and located on two floors. The main jail was on the Superior Street floor, while the boys' division was on the floor above. Offices, including the one used by Commissioner Murian, were also on the upper floor. The station's lowest level, on Michigan Street, emptied into a dirty stretch of waterfront businesses —scrap metal and waste-paper companies, and decrepit warehouses. Here, too, was the station's rear entrance and garage. By 7:45 PM Murnian arrived at the station, mildly shaken at the reception he'd received from crowds of hecklers on the street. "Watch yourself, Murnian!" several youths shouted. "The only thing worse than a *nigger* is a *nigger-lover*!"

Murnian gave no indication he heard the taunting, and was not thwarted in his attempt to get inside the building. He immediately checked to see if any word had come from Chief Murphy, and was visibly upset when told that the chief had called in at 4:45 but had not been heard from since.

Murnian understood the nature of the chief's business in

Virginia, but openly wondered why it was necessary to have both Fiskett and Schulte along too; the only other men in the department with administrative abilities and experience should have remained in town. But now the commissioner, realizing he carried decision-making responsibilities, tried to calm the nervous officers inside the station. He told them everything would work out if they kept their heads. Sgt. Olson, relieved to find himself off the hook with the commissioner's appearance, blurted out, "Nothing's happened yet, anyway."

Murnian, obviously distressed, took Olson aside and asked, "How does it look, Oscar? How many men do you have?"

"Just eleven right now," the sergeant replied. "But more are on the way."

Mark Stewart, a jailer, approached the two and suggested they try to get the blacks out of their cells and up to the county jail. When Murnian didn't respond immediately, Olson said, "I don't know. It's better to be safe than sorry."

Murnian nodded in agreement. "Well, try and keep the sidewalks clear out front," he offered lamely.

"I'll do that," Olson said, moving a few feet away and assigning several men to the front of the building. Then, as an afterthought, he ordered three more to the rear, stationing them in the garage downstairs.

Murnian, growing increasingly agitated as the mob's hooting crescendoed through the closed windows of the station, asked if the chief had indicated when he would return from Virginia. No one knew. Then he shouted for Olson. "Oscar! Can we get the prisoners out anywhere?"

Olson, who was watching the crowds intensify outside, turned to the commissioner. "Chances look slim," he said.

"Well, maybe our best bet is to fight it out here," Murnian said. "Handle it as best you can." The politician must have realized then that whatever occurred during the evening would be on his head. There was no way out. "Do the best you can, Oscar," he repeated, then turned abruptly and went upstairs to his office.

"Jeez, Oscar," one patrolman shouted. "What are we gonna do?"

Olson regarded his men, their faces frozen with the tension of the moment as they understood that they were a minuscule minority compared to the rapidly swelling mobs outside. There was fleeting and murmured conversation about how nobody wanted the confrontation to escalate, and how it would be a damn shame to order police to open fire on their own kind, just to save some "circus niggers."

But the men were police officers sworn to uphold the law. They might have to do what they would have hated and feared at the same time—get rough with white men, friends, and maybe even relatives—to protect the lives of black rapists. One young officer broke for the bathroom, fighting nervous diarrhea. And after a long pause Oscar simply said, "Just keep your heads, boys."

Then he poked his head out front and noticed that perhaps a hundred men were milling about on the Orpheum Theatre corner directly across the street from the station. Olson watched a brief skirmish break out between Harry Sorenson, who was directing traffic on the street, and a youth intent on disrupting the flow of autos. It ended quickly, however, and Olson's mind eased because he wouldn't have to send reinforcements to aid Sorenson, thereby leaving the station further undermanned.

Again the sergeant toyed with the idea of taking the prisoners to some place of safety, but he convinced himself to do so now would be folly. If the blacks were brought outside and somebody grabbed them, the police would be accused of cooperating with the mob.

By 8 PM the switchboard came alive with calls of citizens reporting shooting incidents at various places around the city. Olson, dismissing them as false alarms, sent no one to investigate. Instead, he called his men together. About a dozen sweating, apprehensive men in dark blue uniforms clustered around Olson, casting furtive glances at the windows, their ears tuned to the caterwauling crowd outside.

"Boys, it looks like we might get trouble here," Olson said. "But we can handle it. Let's not have anybody chewing the rag or getting into arguments with those folks on the street. It's best not to talk to anybody. That'll make things worse. Avoid shooting as long as you can. We have almost no ammunition."

At that, most officers checked their bullets, and a few removed clubs from belts. "Me, all I've got in my charge is thirty-one cartridges," Olson went on. "And I don't feel like starting to shoot and lose out on top of it all. But if things get hot, shoot if you have to."

Officers counted bullets again, knowing that each weapon was equipped with only six shots. Their ammunition consisted of barely over a hundred rounds for the entire force on duty. There were, by now, thousands in the mob.

"We'll do the best we can, boys," Olson concluded. Then he stationed six men in front and five at the rear of the station. The time was about ten minutes past eight.

Olson placed a phone call to Fred Johnson, secretary of police, requesting more ammunition. Johnson held the only key to release weapons and ammunition, but Olson wasn't able to hear what Johnson was saying. Groups in the street had merged into a howling mass and had descended upon the station. Johnson's reply was smothered by the crashing of glass as rocks broke through station windows.

During the entire day, Sandra Teale had remained in seclusion at home, sheltered by her mother, who refused to allow visitors into the house. The family was irritated by the furor over the affair, and was probably further aggravated after Dr. Graham had been interviewed by the evening *Herald*. "I believe she is suffering more from nervous exhaustion than anything else," the doctor was quoted as saying.

Another incident, which seemed minor at the time, would later mushroom and spur those congregated around the station downtown. Toward evening a group of passersby called out to Mrs. Teale as she stood on her porch and inquired about Sandra. "She's in bed," Mrs. Teale responded weakly, and rubbed her eyes.

The group, observing Mrs. Teale's hands at her eyes, and hearing the weary, drawn voice, believed the woman told them, "She's dead."

Stunned, the group left the yard and began circulating rumors of Sandra's death around the neighborhoods of West Duluth.

At eight-fifteen that night, in Virginia, the three Duluth officers loaded four black suspects into the backseat of their car. They arranged to have deputies escort six others to Duluth the following morning on the train. No one in Virginia was aware of the trouble in Duluth.

But as they headed out of Virginia, Lt. Schulte became confused on the city's dark streets and took a wrong turn. Thirty minutes passed before he correctly located the Vermilion Road heading back toward Duluth.

In the city, meanwhile, bombardment of the station had picked up intensity, and most windows on the first two floors had been smashed. Even so, the increasing mob had not moved decisively to rush the station, and because of this apparent indecision, Sgt. Olson believed that order could be restored and maintained.

Shortly before eight-thirty, however, about two dozen men made an attempt to gain entrance through the garage downstairs. With Olson leading the charge, six officers, wielding clubs, beat back the halfhearted attack. Patrolman Carl Sundberg, abreast of Olson, chased several attackers back across Michigan Street, hammering away at anyone not moving quickly. Several of his blows made solid connections with shoulders and skulls.

Ironically, the man most battered in this confrontation was William Lashells, who, just moments earlier, had tried to talk the group out of rushing the station. "It's best to let the law take care of it," he had argued. "Besides, property ought to be protected." But he'd been hooted down and had his back turned as Olson and Sundberg led the rush forward.

Sundberg, thinking Lashells was inciting the group, struck him over the head, and Lashells crawled off on hands and knees, finding temporary cover beneath the legs of others as the crowd moved back about thirty yards from the station.

Pleased with the result of the police offensive, Olson returned to the station and rallied his men upstairs. "We beat them in back!" he shouted. "We can take care of it!"

Back downstairs, Sundberg heard someone from outside the station shout, "Wait till the reinforcements get here from West Duluth. You'll have your own hell to pay." And the mob began another charge at the garage.

Aware of the new commotion, Olson hurried back to the rear of the station and down to the garage, where Herman Toewe, a detective, was leading a contingent of four other officers holding the doors. Toewe's foot was against the door in a pathetic attempt to discourage the mob. "Keep your heads, boys," Olson repeated. "I think we'll be okay."

He ran back upstairs, and from a broken window surveyed the roaring mass outside. The once-scattered groups of men, women, and children, now well over five thousand, had suddenly converged, and were surging forward down Superior Street from the west. The sergeant scrambled back inside, dodging a brick that whistled past his jaw. He started to shout an order, but it caught in this throat. My God! he thought. They mean to have the niggers!

TRIAL *by* MOB

At eight-thirty, M Company of the Minnesota National Guard reported for regular Tuesday-night drill at the National Guard Armory at 12th Avenue East and London Road, about a mile east of the station. As the drill was getting under way, several men mentioned seeing the large gathering in front of the jail on their way to the armory.

Capt. L.J. Moerke, commanding officer of the company, sent one of his men downtown to see what was happening. A corporal checked out a motorcycle, drove downtown, and stopped at the Service Motor Company, about fifty feet from the police station entrance. He approached a patrolman and asked if Chief Murphy was present. He was told neither Murphy nor Capt. Fiskett was there, and the corporal gave the patrolman his own name and phone number, telling him in case of trouble the local militia could be called. Then the corporal returned to his unit and informed Moerke that the police thought they could cope with any difficulty. Moerke was cautious, though, and insisted on telling the men that they might have to move if trouble broke out at police headquarters.

Lt. Edward Barber, another veteran police officer on the force, reported for duty shortly after eight-thirty. Inside the station, he found the men confused, but was told that Murnian was in charge. And for a few moments after his arrival there was a lull; the mob was apparently loath to launch an all-out attack on the station, and officers inside the station prematurely believed the worst may have passed. Bricks and other missiles occasionally sailed toward the building, but seemed to be thrown by young boys wanting to get in on the fun.

By eight-forty the mob, now almost ten thousand, was packed throughout the block surrounding the station. Officers in the rear of the station were using clubs to threaten and occasionally beat back some of the front ranks of the mob. It seemed at that time a standoff might be in the making, but to be safe, Sgt. Olson again telephoned Sheriff Magie to request reinforcements.

Magie responded with three deputies and left word for his wife to call the remaining deputies and have them report to police headquarters. Then Magie drove downtown and tried approaching the jail from Second Avenue East, but the street was jammed. He abandoned the car, and with his deputies started toward the station on foot.

In the meantime, Olson had requested assistance from the fire department—only eight blocks from the station, and a truck arrived in minutes, the mob parting for it as it stopped before the station, where firemen connected the hose to a hydrant.

About this time, an order—or rumor of an order—that would tip the balance of power irretrievably in favor of the mob came down from Murnian's third-floor office. That order stated that officers were not to use firearms or clubs on the mob. Murnian, who had generated a following among Duluth laborers, recognized that the mob was substantially comprised of workers. His order must have at least partly stemmed from his feelings for these men. They were not criminals—they were ordinary law-abiding men who were outraged at the alleged

MORNING——The Duluth News Tribune——

...Overpowers ...inst Lynching

—Crude Justice Ad- ...m Seven Three

OPPOSES MOB

ATTA... WAS... NEG...

ATTORNEY HUGH M'CLEARN ATTEMPTS TO STAY MOB

attack on an innocent girl. Nothing could be gained by injuring these men, Murnian reasoned. Olson did not question the order, and felt that the mob could probably be contained with water from the fire hose.

Unknown to officers, and to most of the mob, however, was the activity up on the fire escape between police headquarters and city hall, where a small group of determined young men was vigorously working with drills and chisels, chipping away at the stone wall at the second-floor level. If penetration were possible, they would gain access to the station through the boys' department.

Inside the station, where noise and confusion reigned, police were present and ready to act on orders. But outside the station across the street, someone mounted the hood of a taxicab owned by Joe Zooey. Standing over the mob, with his arms up for attention, he shouted, "The girl assaulted is in critical condition. She's in the hospital if she's not already dead. What would you do if it were your sister? In the South, those niggers would have been dead ten minutes ago!"

Some in the crowd cheered, and raised strips of rope above their heads, and an unidentified speaker picked a strip of rope exhorting, "We're talking about a *white* American girl getting raped by *black* savages and left for dead. What if that girl was your wife or daughter? What would you do? Let's stop yakking!"

Shouts of "Let's get 'em!" echoed from scores of angry throats. The crowd moved toward Second Avenue East, then trampled some of its own men, racing down to Michigan Street, then suddenly turning back up to Superior Street.

Murnian, peering out a window, was spotted by the mob and someone called to him, "We're going to get those niggers, Mr. Murnian! Give us one of them to start with anyway!" The commissioner didn't respond. He stepped back from the window and would remain in relative seclusion for the duration of the assault.

Perhaps realizing that for all practical purposes the police were leaderless, Lt. Barber went to a window. "The prisoners are in my custody," he shouted at the mob. "I am responsible for them. They are guaranteed protection under the law."

"We'll take them from you, Lieutenant," someone answered. "We'll wreck this damn jail and everyone in it."

Barber started to shout back, but a volley of rocks was hurled, and he jumped back, away from the window, unable to complete his appeal.

The mob then rushed the front door for the first time and Patrolman Stewart, standing guard outside the door with Victor Isaacson, was knocked to his knees when a heavy boulder crashed into his shoulder. Isaacson charged Leonard Hedman, as the latter reportedly shouted, "I've got the rope! We want those niggers!" Isaacson shoved Hedman, though several in the mob moved to assist the man. But the officer pressed forward, swinging his massive fists, scattering those in his path.

However, two officers stopped Isaacson and pulled him back to the station. "I could of had him," Isaacson grumbled. "Coulda stopped the thing right now." Puzzled, he retreated to the rear of the station, wondering why officers didn't seem interested in controlling the crowd and thwarting violence.

Patrolman Jacob Nystrom, ministering to the fallen Stewart, heard several men discuss breaking into the hardware store across the street and taking all the guns and ammunition. Then Nystrom was bumped by another rush at the door, and he carried Stewart back inside. But as he did, he caught a stone on the right elbow, rendering his arm useless for the remainder of the battle.

Unable to get water through the first hose, Olson ordered a second one, which was brought by the fire department and hooked up on First Street. Dodging bricks and other missiles, Olson led a five-man police charge to the hose, grappling with the mob at the truck.

The crowd eventually parted for Olson, and jeered him as he climbed on the truck. "Don't let him get that hose," someone shouted, but those few who dared tangle with Olson were easily heaved aside.

Olson stood with the hose momentarily until water started flowing, then he inched back down the hill, spraying the mob as he plowed toward the station. The mob stalled; many were wet and cursing, and a barrage of missiles continued hitting the station.

Olson's men positioned the hose in front of the station and turned the spray around, managing to move the mob back about fifty feet from the station door. But now Olson believed the water was not enough to deter the mob, and he considered requesting the state militia.

At the rear of the station, a railroad iron, employed as a battering ram, punctuated the roar of the mob as it was carried by six men, crashing into and through the large wooden doors, splintering them.

Police manning the hose line were bumped and jostled as the mob grew bolder. While apparently not desiring to battle with officers, the mob couldn't understand why police would make an effort to protect blacks who had raped a white girl. "We're white men too," they repeatedly screamed at police who still kept them slightly at bay with the hundred-foot hose.

Sgt. Olson left the hose after noticing the line of defense give way at the garage as the mob on Superior Street backed off. He experienced a momentary panic; he couldn't be everywhere at once. "Hold 'em boys!" he hollered, dashing back to the rear, only to return quickly out front when the mob moved against the Superior Street doors. He forced his way outside and the size of the mob overwhelmed him. He must have realized that without weapons his case was hopeless—unless he could solicit citizen aid. He walked a half-block west of the station, appealing for help. "This is against the law!" he cried hoarsely. "We need the help of every law-abiding man here!"

Quickly, rudely, he was answered. "The law's no damn good!"

"What'd the law ever do for that girl?"

"We're the law now, mister."

A middle-aged man in a brown suit grabbed Olson, and pulled his florid face very close to the officer's. "What's the matter with you policemen? We're paying you fellows and now you go protecting these *niggers*!"

Olson shoved the man and fought his way back to the station, the ringing jeers of the mob shattering his senses.

"You gonna give us the niggers, Oscar?" a man hollered. "We'll get 'em one way or the other."

"Give 'em up easy, and no one gets hurt," another cried out.

Olson roughly pushed past many men who wouldn't fight him, fearing the sergeant's well-earned reputation as a scrapper. But the mob pressed close behind him, and momentarily it almost looked as if Olson were leading the surge for the front door.

Olson resumed his place on the hose, and ran it into the street, forcing the mob back again. This time, though, the mob was more resolute, and many stood ground, absorbing the soaking as they defiantly waved clubs and ropes at the police. Behind this front line, others renewed a vigorous stone-and-brick assault.

Jacob Nystrom, easing his way outside in another attempt to talk to the mob, was pushed back, his injured arm dangling grotesquely at his side. A man in the mob stood beside the officer. "This man's hurt!" he shouted. "Leave him be!"

Bracing himself against the front of the building, Nystrom tried to gain the attention of the men nearest him. But a young man growled, "How would you like it if it was your sister?" Nystrom shook his head, but the man ignored him and shouted for Murnian. "Are you going to turn those niggers over to us, Mr. Murnian? If you don't, you'll have to have a new police station tomorrow."

"Don't do this," Nystrom pleaded. "These are just boys and they don't know what they're doing."

Inside, Patrolman Bill McKenna wondered aloud why the police weren't using weapons. "For God's sake, we should get out the rifles!" he shouted near the jailer's desk. "No good, Bill," one hollered back. "That'd be real trouble."

Downstairs, Isaacson raised his pistol as the assault heightened at the garage door. "Don't shoot!" several in the mob shouted, and the cry was hastily seconded by another officer. "No shooting!" he cried.

About a dozen from the mob were inside the garage now, and those out on Michigan Street rushed the doors again with the battering ram, springing the hinges; one door opened and hung at a tilt as the undeterred crowd scrambled forward.

TRIAL *by* MOB

By eight-fifty the mob was larger and angrier than it had been just thirty minutes earlier. Many in the crowd were now withstanding the force of water from the police hose, and continued heaving rocks at the station. Sgt. Olson determined that police would need additional hoses, and he made another request of the fire department. But congestion on Superior Street was so thick that the fire truck was unable to penetrate the mass, and the crew had to stop at Second Avenue East and First Street. The truck was immediately surrounded by the mob, and some of the crowd began scuffling with firemen.

Nystrom, though pained and partially crippled by injury, tried to help other officers get the hose off the truck. But he was easily moved away by men in the mob who told him to stay out of it—that he was already hurt and they didn't want to see things worsen for him.

Two dozen men had pushed forward and started wrestling with officers for the hose. Nystrom pressed on, his left hand clenching his club, but Louis Dondino shoved him and growled, "Don't you *dare* touch that hose! Those men are doing good work!"

Easily overpowering police, the mob took the hose off the truck and ran it back to a hydrant on the corner, then hurried it down the hill and pointed it at the front of the station. However, they were unable to get immediate water pressure, and those manning the hose were given another forceful dousing by police. Two men in front were knocked down by the stream of water.

As the mob abandoned the fire truck, firemen returned to their station and secured more hoses. But this time no officers were able to meet the truck, and the third hose was virtually handed to the mob. This time the mob turned bursts of water against the police. When the spray hit, the police retreated into the station, followed by water and a hail of bricks.

Inside the station, many officers began asking whether the blacks were worth this battering. Handicapped by not having access to firearms and clubs, police realized that unless reinforcements came through, it was only a matter of time before the mob would have its way.

Leo E. Streetar, the city editor and night editor of *The News Tribune*, managed to get inside the station after being recognized by Lt. Barber. Streetar had been a police reporter for over two years with the *Minneapolis News*, and was more in his element here than any other Duluth reporter. The only reporter with big city experience, he, more than other reporters, understood the horrible consequences that likely would result from the absence of decisive police action.

Soaked himself, and trying to get a pencil to write on his waterlogged notebook paper, he drew Barber aside and asked what the lieutenant was going to do. "There isn't a hell of a lot we *can* do," Barber said. He was exhausted, his eyes swollen, reddened slits from the water he had taken when the mob turned hoses on police.

Two men in front were pointing a hose at the station and were running it closer. "Why don't you pinch those two?" Streetar asked. But Barber shook his head. "I'm afraid if we do, they'll start a riot."

"This is a riot already!" Streetar screamed. "What about using your guns?"

"No, we can't," Barber said. "We'll start real trouble if we do."

Streetar asked about the advisability of getting the National Guard, but Barber moved off, and the reporter started up the soaked, slippery stairs to see Commissioner William Murnian.

When Joseph Payer arrived for duty, he was not in uniform, and the attack on the station was already under way. The mob was jammed in around the the front of the building, so he ran down to Michigan Street, where Bill Rozon was guarding the back street door for the mob. Payer gained entrance there because Rozon didn't spot him as an officer.

In the chaos, Payer received no direct orders, and found the entire station in disarray. He wandered upstairs, where hammering on the wall could be heard, over the clamor of the mob below and outside. Payer located a fireman's ax and put it under his coat, then slipped out again and made his way through the crowd up to the hydrant on Second Avenue. With one swing of the ax he severed one of the mob's hoses, then dashed away before he was noticed.

Again a temporary advantage returned to police, and some officers believed a show of force, the firing of weapons, would bring the mob to its knees. But under Murnian's restrictions, most officers had already lost their stomach for battle. One by one they dropped off their hose, until only Sgt. Olson remained with it.

Other police, battered and drenched, retreated to the secretary's room inside headquarters and took refuge from water and bricks. Demoralized and defeated, they sat stunned, nursing wounds and scrounging dry matches for damp cigarettes. Still others, fearing imminent break-in by the full mob, hurried to the basement, where protection seemed more secure.

Alone on the hose, Sgt. Olson considered drawing his weapon, but held back because he wasn't sure how many, if any, of his men would assist him once the shooting started. That he would kill or injure someone by firing point-blank into the mob was a certainty. But Olson was one cop who resorted to the gun only as a last resort.

Still, he held fast to the hose, and was managing to keep the crowd back a bit in front, though some men were gaining entrance at Michigan Street.

Harry Sorenson, a traffic officer, had remained on his corner, attempting to reroute traffic on Superior Street, but as vehicles and pedestrians clogged the street, he found the situation impossible, and started back to the station. As he approached it, he saw two officers attempting to wrestle the hose from the mob. They were taking some punches, and Sorenson hustled to their aid, pushing two men and shouting, "Drop that hose in the name of the law!"

His order ignored, he was struck from behind with a club. Groping to his feet, he managed to grab on to Olson's hose, and he stayed with the sergeant until the mob directed its other hose at the officers. Sorenson caught a stream full in the face and floundered off the hose, unable to breathe. Someone with a piece of jagged metal slashed at him, tearing a large wound in his leg. Barely able to see, Sorenson staggered back to the station, where he was taken to the jailer's room. Several minutes passed before he regained normal breathing after paroxysms of coughing and spitting.

Back out front, someone in the mob finally cut Olson's hose, and the water abruptly dwindled to a trickle, leaving the hefty officer standing alone before the mob, his uniform drenched, his body bruised.

He dropped the hose and backed toward the station, almost daring someone to step forward. Wisely, perhaps, the mob waited until Olson had disappeared behind the front doors, and then encouraged, rushed the door, joined by those who had until then merely been spectators.

The front door quickly gave way, and dozens poured through, stumbling and brawling in their zeal to get inside and into the cells. At the same time, a few men kept hammering at the splintered doors with abandoned sledgehammers. And some younger boys happily picked up crowbars and randomly whacked at the walls of the station.

As the mob roared past him and began working on the cell room door, Olson made his way back to the secretary's room. His eyes bloodshot and tear-stained, he looked at his men "Boys, what're we gonna do?" he asked in a voice raw and hoarse.

No one responded. None of the others were looking at Olson, and faintly, officers could hear the muffled frightened sobs of a black prisoner.

At nine forty-five, Duluth theaters emptied into Superior Street, and these theatergoers now joined the throng moving rapidly toward the station. Ladies in evening finery, clutching the arms of their escorts, urged them to press closer for a better look at what was happening.

Carl Sundberg, who had been on duty outside the station, returned to headquarters and rushed to the side of Lt. Barber, who was hunched over, retching. Barber saw Sundberg, and straightened up. "Carl, let's go in and see what we can do," he said weakly. The two headed for Michigan Street, and tried to push in at the garage entrance, but found it too jammed with people. They returned to Superior Street and finally found themselves inside, clearing a partial entry by fighting off several men from the mob. They worked their way to the middle of the packed hall, yet some distance from the cell room. As they started to squeeze past, men hollered, "Block them! Block them!" And dozens, some grinning, enjoying the spectacle, shoved back, pushing the officers against a wall, where they were pinned.

Barber was hoisted by the mob, carried on their shoulders and brought to the grilled door of the cell room, where men demanded the cell keys and tore at Barber's clothes in a vain effort to find them.

Sundberg freed himself during the preoccupation with Barber and latched another officer, Stans Nesgoda. "Let's go and see if we can do something for Barber," he said. "He's up against it." The officers forged through the mass, moving about five yards, but were pushed back. One man warned them not to interfere. "Don't try to protect these black savages!" he screamed.

Sundberg grabbed him. "You should be ashamed of yourself. You've hardly left school, and you come and do such a thing."

"When cops start using clubs to beat their own race, that's when something is wrong," Sundberg was told. Then the officer was spun back and thrown against a wall as Hank Stephenson advanced on him with a raised sledgehammer. But the burly Sundberg glared at the man until the weapon was lowered. Sundberg again tried to persuade those nearest him to quit the fight, but Stephenson returned again and, backed by six or seven others bearing crowbars and hammers, shouted, "Get out of here!" while menacing Sundberg with his hammer.

The officer tripped and reeled into a jagged edge on the door of the cell room. Waves of pain ripped through his right leg and he fell. Nesgoda steadied him, but was warned, "Both of you keep going. There are two men right back of you, and they have a gun. Both of them."

As the patrolmen gingerly picked their way back through the crowded entry and out onto the street, Sundberg was struck in the small of the back with a brick, and toppled to the sidewalk.

TRIAL *by* MOB

From his Michigan Street office, Fred Beecher heard the mob's screaming and hooting increase, and his feelings dissolved into thoughts that there probably would be a lynching in the city. He left the office and arrived at the police station around 9:30 PM. By this time the demolition of headquarters had begun, while an almost endless crowd poured through the entrance and filled the Superior Street hallway.

Maintaining the resolute bearing of a military commander, Beecher sidled through the crowd, brushing against many men, surreptitiously running his hands against coat pockets. Though a few seemed to have handguns, Beecher still believed that for a mob of this size it was extremely orderly. And he wondered why police were unable to control such a mob.

He observed many who were tossing bricks or plying crowbars to doors, and paused to explain to newsmen or other bystanders what they were doing. And though boisterous, the mob impressed Beecher as one that would probably not wantonly kill innocent men. Still, a mob is totally unpredictable. Angry now, but with appropriate stimulation, the mob's anger could quickly turn to maddened frenzy.

Beecher was uncertain what action he'd personally take at that point, when he heard someone holler, "We better get in there and get 'em quick. Or they'll have the National Guard out here!" Beecher dashed away and tried to find a telephone. But none was in service near headquarters, so he ran back to his own office and asked the long-distance operator if she knew whether troops had been called. She replied that such information was confidential and could not be released. Beecher identified himself as a major with the Fourth Field Artillery; the operator connected him with her supervisor, who told him no troops had been summoned.

Beecher placed calls to the state adjutant general, W.F. Rhinow, and to Maj. Harry Brady, Col. George Leach, and Col. Harry Bellows. Brady, Leach, and Bellows were former associates of Beecher's in Minneapolis; Bellows, Beecher's former commanding officer, was an expert on riot-control tactics. Leach, who the next year would be elected as a conservative mayor of Minneapolis, advised Beecher that city officials must first formally request assistance before the Guard could step in. Leach suggested that Rhinow be informed, and Beecher said he had already called the general but couldn't reach him. In the meantime, Beecher asked, was there anything that could be done?

Leach wasn't sure, but told Beecher to keep close watch on developments. Then at 9:55 PM Gen. Rhinow, on duty at the state encampment at Fort Snelling, returned Beecher's call and repeated what Leach had said about city officials having to make formal request for troops. Beecher contacted Sheriff Magie, who joined him at the Michigan Street office, and the two phoned Gen. Rhinow. Rhinow ordered Beecher on active duty, and said troops would be up on the first available train. Beecher assured the general that he would take charge of making necessary arrangements for the troop arrival in Duluth, then he and the sheriff hurried back to the jail.

Though the mob continued pouring into the jail, a young photographer was allowed to set up his tripod in order to photograph the event. But when Magie and Beecher arrived on the scene, the photo session broke up. "All over, Sheriff," someone hollered. "Might as well go home to bed."

Beecher and Magie forced their way through the crowd at the jail door, where they saw a group of men hammering against the cell-room door. The mob around them chanted, "Ho—ho—ho—" with each ring of the hammers. Murnian was standing unobtrusively near this scene, and was spotted by Magie. The sheriff tried to get the commissioner's attention, and he called, "What should we be doing?" But Murnian did not seem to notice the sheriff, and melted into the mob.

"They got more of the black bastards up to Virginia!" a young man shouted. "What are we waiting for?" another yelled. "Let's get up there!"

Magie panicked. The prisoners were in custody of his deputies. Magie picked his way through the mob and returned to his office at the county jail, and phoned Virginia to warn of a possible contingent from Duluth coming up to get the remaining blacks. He was told that Murphy had already taken four prisoners with him back to Duluth, leaving for the city shortly after 8 PM. However, six blacks were still in the Virginia jail, and were to be escorted down on the morning train.

"Be careful." warned Magie. "These people mean business."

Deputies in the small town of Virginia anticipated a nightmare. Within the hour, a rumor filtered through the population that a caravan of fifty cars, loaded with armed men, was headed for Virginia to take the rest of the blacks. Law-enforcement personnel there numbered fewer than a dozen, and the likelihood of citizens assisting the law officers in such an occurrence looked doubtful; nobody was going to stick his neck out for "niggers"—maybe not even the officers. Said one of the deputies, "We'll post a watch on the Vermilion Road, and say our prayers."

The mob working at the Duluth jail maintained such remarkable order that many observers would later believe the incident had been a well-planned attack by the Wobblies from the IWW, or even the Communists.

Attorney Hugh McClearn, a raspy-voiced rustic, a favorite among his peers for his wit and charm, had stayed at the scene after Judges Cant and Fesler left. As hammers rang and saws whined and screeched, almost muted by the crowd's increasing bedlam, McClearn mounted a rickety stepladder in the stifling hallway. His gray-streaked hair matted with sweat, McClearn pleaded with the mob to stop.

Gradually, the disenchanted mutterings ceased, but not before two men attempted to shake McClearn from the ladder. Edward McDevitt, an assistant county attorney, angrily shoved the two away and steadied the ladder. Though the work of hammers continued, the hundreds packed in the cell hall listened to McClearn.

"Give the courts a chance to administer justice according to the law," he cried, his voice cracking. "Sgt. Olson says there are six niggers here. Three of the men the police have no dope on at all. They may be absolutely innocent."

"If we get the ropes, we'll find the guilty ones soon enough!" someone retorted.

McClearn steadied himself on the ladder. The temperature in the hallway had risen to over ninety degrees, and the stench of sweat was all pervasive. "Men, I—"

"We don't care if they are guilty or innocent!" a man yelled. "Kill the black snakes!"

"Wait!" McClearn pleaded, his hands over his head, waving for silence, but he could not hear his own voice above the renewed clamoring. "Look, boys, I'm as indignant about the attack on the girl as you are. But the proper thing to do is to leave the law take its course."

The mob quieted after someone shouted, "You a lawyer, Mister?"

"We don't have no electric chair or hanging in Minnesota, ain't that right?"

Sadly, the lawyer shook his head. "No, but—"

"Then what happens to the niggers, lawyer?"

McClearn would remember he'd have given anything at that moment to be able to tell the mob that conviction for rape meant death or even life in prison. He would later say that if the men could have been assured of that, they may well have ceased. But after he struggled for a deep breath, he said, "If they're convicted, they'll get five to thirty years."

"To hell with the law!" screamed several dozen men. And McClearn was roughly pulled from the ladder. McDevitt, however, mounted the ladder and started a brief speech, asking the men to use reason, telling them that they themselves would have to stand trial for what they were doing.

"No red-blooded man would convict anyone here tonight!" a middle-aged man screamed, shoving the ladder.

Then Oscar Olson climbed the ladder, the steps sagging under his great weight. He spotted a man. "Look, fellow," he began, his voice reduced to slightly more than a whisper. "We don't even know if we got the right Negroes. That circus had nearly two hundred of them, and we arrested thirteen. And the girl and her young man couldn't identify a single one."

"The girl might be dead."

"Let's wait ten minutes and check it out," Olson argued. "Ten minutes!"

"No! She's in critical condition if she isn't already dead."

Olson reached toward the young man. "They listen to you.

Speak for law and order. Tell them to go home."

Instead, the reply Olson received was that the men wanted justice done, and someone, then a lot of someones, shouted, "Let's go! Let's go!"

TRIAL *by* MOB

ater was running ankle-deep over the floor of the jail as the mob and officers sloshed through it. Their bodies were pressed together in frenzied, frenetic movement, and men fell and were trampled by the mass rushing through. The heat and stench overcame some, and they vomited where they fell.

Several more officers simply retired to the basement to tend minor wounds, and were joined by Oscar Olson, who moments earlier had been threatened with lynching himself for interfering with the mob. "Jeez, Oscar," moaned one of the men, "you done the best you could."

But Olson was not ready to quit. "Come on, boys," he urged, clapping a raw hand on a young patrolman's shoulder. "We'll run out the back way, up the hill, and take the hose away from the mob."

The men regarded their haggard sergeant in glassy-eyed silence, and shook their heads. The man was crazy, they must have thought. For one hundred and fifteen dollars a month, a man risks his life for a bunch of niggers? Not for a lousy one hundred and fifteen dollars, he doesn't, not when he's supposed to be fighting white men—

men of his own race. It just didn't make sense.

Olson tried again to encourage his men, then heaved a helpless shrug when the men failed to respond. They had tried. They did their duty. Now they were tired. Tired and defeated. None could look at Olson as he went back upstairs to continue efforts to halt the onslaught.

Herman Toewe, a detective who never shunned a brawl, an officer who occasionally challenged the man he was arresting to slug it out, a man who prided himself on never having used his gun and who boasted he hadn't met the man he couldn't take with his fists, had, with other officers, flinched in the face of the mob's attack. It wasn't right, he obviously reasoned, to fight your own kind.

But around 10 PM, when he noticed four men heading for the detective's office, known as the Bertillon Room, he was quick to act. The Bertillon Room was the private sanctuary of detectives, the elite of the Duluth force. And Toewe was proud of being a detective. It always gave him a special lift to pass the desk out front, where the uniformed boys sipped coffee from mugs and spilled crumbling sandwiches in their laps, and stroll into the efficient tranquillity of the Bertillon Room.

Now the mob meant to go in and muddy that room, and perhaps turn the hose on it. But not while Herm Toewe was around. "Hey!" he shouted. "There's nobody in there!"

"We'll see for ourselves!" a man said.

Toewe, being hopelessly outnumbered and not desiring combat now, tried to hold his ground. "Look, if you'll detail one man, I'll take him in here and turn on the lights and leave him to look around to satisfy you there are no niggers in there." The men agreed.

Cautiously, Toewe inserted the key in the lock and allowed the representative inside, slipping in behind him and snapping on the lights. The delegate glanced around. Toewe was no doubt pleased the floor still held a trace of shine. "Okay," the man said finally. "Thanks."

"It's okay," Toewe said, and as they left, he carefully relocked the door.

Lt. Barber had also been threatened with lynching. He was told that while the mob was only after the "niggers," they'd take "nigger-lovers," too. And another man approached Barber with a hammer, and snarled. "We're going to lynch those niggers. What would you do if it was your sister?"

Barber backed off, went outside, and tried speaking to women in the crowd, asking them to help him persuade husbands and boyfriends to leave. He noticed baby carriages and dozens of young children prancing about. Other youngsters were being held aloft on shoulders of parents for a better look. The officer was aghast that adults would bring children to such a spectacle.

Caught in a momentary reverie, perhaps due to extreme exhaustion, Barber felt he was no longer part of the struggle and seemed to be more of an outside observer. But the sharp explosion of the mob's hose brought him back to reality when it struck him full in the face. He couldn't see for a moment as his eyes rapidly swelled.

He started back inside, pushing through the crowd. He stepped inside the door and fell, his strength sapped by heat, humidity, and the battering he'd absorbed. The stink of his wet wool uniform rose to his nostrils, and he fought a swoon before being lifted by several young men and again pinned against a wall.

10:20 PM—Despite the deeply rooted fundamentalist religious faith of many southern blacks, none of the arrested circus employees had previously espoused any faith. Now, however, one—Isaac McGhie—tried. Almost oblivious of the quiet terror of his mates,

McGhie rocked back and forth on his knees, tears rolling down his cheeks. "Help me, Jesus . . . help me, Jesus. Lord Jesus, please help me," he pleaded hysterically. The other prisoners neither looked to Jesus, nor anywhere else for help. There was among them now an increased apprehension of doom.

10;55 PM—Albert W. Tracy, the automobile editor of *The Duluth Herald*, would have been home in bed. But since the paper's staff was depleted due to vacations and illnesses, Tracy had been assigned double duty, adding the city hall beat to his regular reporting. It was not an assignment he relished. The city hall beat, while often earning writers front-page stories, was, in most ways, routine. The mayor issued proclamations, and regularly met with the commissioners, occasionally decided on zoning ordinances, or purchased new equipment for the public works department. But there hadn't been any real excitement at the meetings since the summer of 1917, when the wet/dry issue was first debated.

On the other hand, the automobile was new. It excited folks. People were thinking that almost anyone could own an auto and experience the thrill of speeding down the road at twenty-five, maybe thirty, miles an hour. Why, a man could load his family into the flivver, drive down to see his brother in Minneapolis, and make the 160-mile trip in less than a day.

As automobile editor, Tracy was treated with the respect due an authority, an expert, and he received much mail from readers. Many wanted him to help them buy their cars, and while he never agreed to do it, he was flattered by the attention. He had as much prestige as any sports columnist, and was well known about town. And until this night, his assessment of the city hall beat had proven correct.

At 11 PM he was upstairs with Commissioner Murnian, asking him pointed questions. "The officers say somebody gave orders not to shoot," Tracy said. "Was it you?"

Murnian was weary. Exhaustion mapped his face, and his body sank into his desk chair in defeated surrender. Politically, he was a man between a rock and a hard place. No matter what happened, he had to accept some major responsibilities for this evening. But Duluth was a white city, and he'd been elected by white voters who would go to the polls again next year.

Tracy persisted. "Did you give that order, Mr. Murnian?"

Despite his exhaustion, Murnian was angry. Void of energy, he looked at the reporter and in a measured monotone replied, "I do not want to see the blood of one white person spilled for six blacks."

Tracy stared at the commissioner, then jotted down the quote. He repeated the statement and asked Murnian to verify its accuracy.

Murnian couldn't be sure what he said, but he wished that the reporter were out of his office, away from him, and he nodded and dismissed Tracy with a resigned wave of hand.

Out on the Vermilion Road, a solitary car joggled toward Duluth at just under twenty miles an hour. In the back seat, cramped together, four blacks stared impassively at the dark landscape, broken by scrubby poplars and spruce, or tried to sleep. In the front were the three officers, stifling yawns, twisting irritably when stricken with leg cramps. The police were not in a speaking mood, and any attempt by the blacks at conversation merited a sharp "Shut up!" from the officers.

Schulte, still behind the wheel, guessed they should arrive downtown a little before midnight. He noticed a road sign advertising a resort on Rice Lake, near the city. Suddenly, he broke the silence. "I got a funny feeling," he said. "You don't suppose something's up downtown?"

The other two remarked that while it was possible, it was not probable. At least they hoped not.

When Public Works Commissioner Bert Farrell first became aware of the attack at the jail, he went downtown and kept a vigilant eye on the action for over an hour. About 9:30 PM word reached him that a group was going to Virginia to get the rest of the blacks. Then Farrell left downtown and drove out on the Vermilion Road, hoping to head off Chief Murphy on his return to the city.

At 10:45 PM he left his car and stood in the middle of the road, flagging down oncoming cars. Three were false alarms before the police auto approached and pulled over. "Trouble, John," Farrell shouted, huffing over to the police vehicle. "Hell's poppin' in Duluth. They're going to lynch the prisoners. Supposed to be a bunch headed to Virginia, too."

Murphy asked when mob activity started downtown and whether Murnian had taken precautions. Farrell didn't know what Murnian had done, but repeated that the situation was completely out of hand. "You can't take these men to town now," he said, referring to the prisoners. "The thing to do is leave them with me. I can get hold of some fellas and we'll hide them at my place overnight."

Stunned, the chief agreed, and issued arms to Farrell, then escorted the blacks to Farrell's farm about two miles down the road before the three officers made their frantic dash for town.

The grilled door to the cell room remained under heavy attack from the cheering men manning the railroad iron ram in relays. Eagerly, each man in turn took a position on the ram as it clanked against the grille, finally breaking through in spots, gouging jagged tears in the twisted steel.

A few citizens and officers offered impotent pleas to go home, but these efforts only intensified the mob's determination. Shouts of "Kill 'em!" rang out over the clanging of the iron.

Lt. Barber, his uniform soaked, ripped, and dirtied, made

several more attempts to wrench the battering ram from the mob, but was thrown back and tossed into the air before moving off.

Some of the mob still worked outside, where they had first outflanked the officers by climbing the fire escape to the city hall next door. They had since hammered through sixteen inches of brick and mortar, forging a hole three feet wide and two feet high through the wall. Dozens more crowded through this entrance and joined the attack on the grille.

The prisoners inside the darkened cell room had been utterly alone. During the early part of the evening, when the rumble began, they were heard shouting for help. But as the battle for the station progressed, they remained silent, except for an occasional sob or mumbled prayer.

Most alone of the prisoners was twenty-year-old Isaac McGhie, who had been sequestered in a cell on the second floor boys' division. There had been no one with whom he could talk, no human voice to cry with or to issue reassurances. And in the darkness there, the young man was consumed with panic.

At least the others downstairs had each other. There was, perhaps, some small comfort in that. And, perhaps, they could say to each other that since they were up north, they really didn't have anything to worry about. But those reassurances must have sounded hollow, indeed, when the rage and fury of the mob could be so clearly heard up to a mile away.

Though uneducated, and mainly from sharecropping families in the South, the blacks were no strangers to lynch law. The law was universal in much of the South—no black could ever contaminate the flesh of a white woman without paying with his own life. Lynching was a grisly scene too often repeated; in fact, the circus blacks, when signing on, would have been warned by older black hands that they were under no circumstance to bother with white women. Even up north. The circus, nor anybody else, would be able to give them much help if they got into that sort of trouble.

It was a warning usually well-heeded. But, regardless of that warning, these six men were under arrest, suspected of raping a white girl. Though they might not have realized it then, their only hope was that they were in one of the northernmost cities in America, a city where racial animosities were virtually unheard of.

Even that faint hope was being rapidly destroyed by the fevered activities of the mob. And when the attack was launched on cell-room doors, the prisoners whispered among themselves that they would hide under their cots praying that they couldn't be seen, and hope against hope that the mob might think they had been moved.

The blacks, trembling, took their pathetic positions upon hearing the jubilant and victorious yelp as the grilled door was finally sprung, and hundreds surged into the dark room.

TRIAL *by* MOB

Cursing groups of men parted in diverting streams, circling about the cells. "Where are they?" men were shouting, upon first believing the cells were empty. "They up to county jail?"

Apparently the attack on the building had resulted in a partial power failure, for there was no electricity in the cell room, and the first wave of searchers was not equipped with flares.

"Police have lied to us!" several shouted, giving the first indication that perhaps some officers had cooperated with the mob by telling the men that the prisoners were locked in cells in the jail.

"We'll find the niggers if we have to go to hell for them!" another shouted, and the rush pressed on throughout the cell room.

After about five minutes a flare was struck, briefly illuminating the corridor with an eery red brilliance, but its carrier fell, and the flare was doused by the inch-deep water on the floor.

Four other police officers, meanwhile, started for the cellroom, hoping to assist Lt. Barber, but the mob turned on them, taking up the cry, "Crowd them out! Crowd them out!" These police were quickly surrounded by the jostling that pushed them back to the cell-room entrance. And Lt. Barber, released as the crowd began the search of cells, continued his plea. "Stop this before you murder innocent men!"

"We don't care if they are innocent or not!" someone yelled, showering spittle in the officer's face.

One man, however, thought to take a closer look. He shoved through to the first cell, peered in, straining to accustom his eyes to the darkness. He started to back away in disgust, but lurched forward again, discovering a human form rolled into a bundle, huddled in the dark next to the wall on the floor beneath the cot. "There's one!" he cried, and immediately the crowd was at the cell, battering and sawing through the bars in a frantic effort to reach the prisoner.

The prisoner was nineteen-year-old Loney Williams. But the maddened mob kept on hammering and cursing, and Williams finally crawled from his hiding place and sat on his cot, cradling his head in his hands. His lips formed a silent prayer before he vomited.

The mob crushed forward, though this pressure hindered its progress on the cell bars. Still, there was a willingness to assist within the mob, and as one man became fatigued from pounding or sawing, another was quick to take his place.

Above the din, Lt. Barber, tears streaming from his eyes, cried out, "You are going to be sorry for this night's work! These men would be punished by the law! You are doing wrong! *Stop*, before it's too late!" But, instead, the mob redoubled its efforts. Several from the mob with whom Barber was acquainted went to him and tried convincing him that his work was no use. "It's out of the hands of police," one told him.

"But I am responsible for these men," he half sobbed. "The chief is at Virginia, the chief of detectives, the captain—all of them are with him. I am in charge here and I'm going to prevent this if I can."

But Barber was only talking to himself. None in the mob was listening, and the cry arose again, "Get 'em! Kill the black sons of bitches!"

Upstairs in the boys' division, Isaac McGhie was found and removed from his cell, absorbing a vicious beating by the mob as he was shoved downstairs and placed in custody of mob leaders. McGhie, as he was thrown against a wall and pummelled once more, spit out a tooth and gingerly covered a broken nose. He stood for a moment, petrified at the fury of the mob, and for the first time since infancy, he urinated in his pants.

"We've got 'em now," chorused the crowd as Williams's cell was hammered in. By this time the other prisoners had been discovered, and their cells were under attack. Slowly, the blacks crawled from beneath cots and sat on them, dolefully regarding the mob.

McGhie began to wring his hands. His gold-filled tooth flashed in the glancing light of flares, and his eyes rolled wretchedly. "Oh, God, oh, God—oh, God," he repeated. "I am only twenty years old. I have never done anything wrong. I swear I didn't. Oh, God, my God, help me."

Another prisoner, Elmer Jackson, stood beside his cot and observed with apparent curiosity the vigorous attempts to open his cell, first by battering at the hinges, then at the lock and finally on the trapdoor overhead through which prisoners were fed. While the mob managed to rip several bars and fastenings, they couldn't make a large enough opening fast enough to suit those behind them. Several fistfights erupted within the mob as men tried to assume direction of the break-in.

Another prisoner, John Thomas, stood at his cell door and argued with the mob. "Nobody here done nothin'," he said calmly as the crowd pushed close and tried to reach him through the bars with hands and chisels.

"You niggers'll swing! Every damn one of you!" they cried.

Thomas stood farther back in his cell, his arms folded over his chest. "We ain't done nothin'," he insisted again.

The mob backed off Thomas's cell as the chorus of cheers exploded two cells down. The cell of nineteen-year-old Elias Clayton had been forced open, and two men entered and punched Clayton to the floor, but others pulled them back. McGhie was dragged into Clayton's cell, and three whites stood guard, keeping others away form the prisoners. "We're going to find out which nigger's guilty!" one man shouted. "The rest of you stay back. We want to be fair!"

A weird semblance of order unfolded when several more whites were allowed into the cell, while another three were posted outside with orders to keep everyone back until the examination was completed. "We'll get to the bottom of this!" called one of the vigilante jurors. Inside the cell, along with the blacks and several other whites, were Nate Natelson, Hank Stephenson, and John Burr.

The roaring of the mob was subsiding as other blacks were removed from their cells and herded into the one cell where the "trial" was about to begin. The six blacks, beaten and bloodied, viewed the swarm of hostile faces from the cramped, humid cell. As one tried to turn toward the mob, he was punched, his head slamming into the cell bars.

Orders were randomly barked at the confused, battered prisoners. "Turn around when we're talking to you."

"Now, which one of you did it? Out with it—"

"Who was the one with the gun?"

"Come on, talk—damn you!"

The prisoners, dazed, unable to respond, could only stare at the inquisitors, perhaps not even comprehending the bizarre horror crashing about them. "Never mind the questions—let's just kill these niggers!" someone hollered.

"The militia will be here before we can hang 'em."

"Okay, we want only the guilty man," shouted one of the jurors. "So, who did it?"

"So help me, God, I did nothing and I know nothing," screamed a weeping Isaac McGhie. And the rest of the blacks desperately denied any guilt or even knowledge of who might have been involved. "The miserable black savages are lying," men shouted.

It became impossible for "investigators" to obtain connected stories from the prisoners since the noise prohibited coherence. And the impatience of the hundreds in the cell room could no longer be suppressed.

John Burr, who found his early opposition to the attack on the jail dissolving during the passionate heat of mob activity, began to realize the tragic wrong taking place. From his vantage point inside the cell, he vowed that at least no innocent black would be seized.

Loney Williams, whose bland expression seemed to convey a touch of arrogance, was the only black wearing polished brown boots. Many in the mob pressed toward him, reaching through the bars, grasping at him, shouting, "Give us boots! . . . Give us boots!" But Burr jumped in front of Williams and tried to calm the mob. "No, leave him be. This boy has a good story," Burr shouted. Williams stationed himself directly behind Burr, keeping the white man between himself and the mob.

"Give us *somebody*!" the mob screamed. Pale and sweating, many inquisitors were ready to give up. "Hell, get 'em out of here," one of them said as several in the jury were helped outside, overcome by suffocating heat and humidity.

A man grabbed McGhie, who was nearest the cell door, by the hair and the black fell to his knees. "No—please—" he begged, only to be jerked up and thrust out of the cell door into the eager hands of the mob, and Elmer Jackson was shoved after him. The mob howled and immediately set upon the two, beating, kicking, spitting, and cursing as McGhie and Jackson were forced through a narrow opening of the cell-room door and led out before the wild and shrieking mass on Superior Street.

McGhie and Jackson were literally thrown from hands to hands; their shirts and jackets ripped until the the two were naked to the waist. By the time they were across Superior Street, their pitiful whimpers were submerged under the savage roar of the mob. While neither man struggled, McGhie went limp and seemed to faint. Someone hoisted him up and several punched him down again.

Among the many women outside the station, one aged nineteen or twenty held no sympathy for the mob. Standing beside the door of the jail in a blue tailored suit that was dripping from water sprayed by police and the mob, she viciously cursed both factions in the struggle. Men attempted to drag her out of the way as water splashed over her clothing, but she refused to move, a lone civilian voice virtually drowned under by the intense screeching of the mob. She reached toward McGhie in a feeble rescue attempt, but she was immediately thrown back and enveloped by a large man in a gray coat, who held her.

McGhie was dragged, begging for his life, up Second Avenue East. Jackson, his head down, bobbing and dodging the punches and kicks aimed at him, remained silent. As the two were brought up the hill, many in the mob fought each other for the chance to take a swing or kick at the prisoners. Women in high heels kicked and stomped at the helpless men until the procession was stopped in front of the Shrine Auditorium at Second Avenue East and First Street.

Inside the building, Duluth Shriners were preparing for a trip to Portland, Oregon. Attracted by the intense crescendo outside, they peered from their second-floor perch as the grim tableau was formed. There, thousands of cursing, screaming Duluthians were dragging and beating two young blacks up the avenue where scores of others were gathered beneath the light pole on the corner.

Albert Johnson, the accountant, had seen Dondino's truck earlier that day and suspected something might take shape downtown. The talk of the West Duluth gang going down to take the blacks was more than just talk—it was going to happen. And like thousands of others, Johnson went downtown and watched as the mob attacked the jail. As soon as he saw the blacks come out, he hurried up to First Street and climbed a light pole, anticipating a better vantage point to see the hanging. Near the top, he gripped the arm that extended over the street on which the light was fastened. Men from the mob below were removing sections of rope, and the heads of the two blacks bobbed and ducked punches which were still leveled at them. Suddenly, Johnson's heart caught. His bowels felt moist. The men dragging the blacks swerved from the opposite corner and brought them to the foot of the very pole young Johnson had climbed. Below him, many in the mob were chanting and singing. There was some laughter, but most faces were angry, serious. Johnson could see the petrified Isaac McGhie glance up, his lithe dark body stripped to the waist. McGhie's face was bloody, and he was trembling.

"Toss this rope over the top, kid!" someone hollered at Johnson, casting a sturdy length of new rope to him. The youth froze momentarily as the rope looped over his arm. It probably occurred to him that he was irretrievably involved—no longer a mere observer. He held the rope that would take the lives of the blacks, and even if these were colored boys, did they deserve to die like this? Johnson looked at the rope. His fingers felt thick, numb, and useless. He looked down at the crowd, at the blacks. His ears were ringing as he saw the open throats of perhaps thousands of others screaming epithets at the blacks. Frightened and intimidated, Johnson knew he was going to commit a grave wrong, but he did as he was told, cinching the rope over the light pole. And as the mob howled its approval, nineteen-year-old Albert Johnson shuddered violently.

WOOD BRANDS PREST. BUTLER'S S

The Duluth

DULUTH MOB

When The Mob Dragged Forth It

WOOD BRANDS BUTLER'S WORDS MALICIOUS LIE

MENT AS MALICIOUS FALSEHOOD

ws Tribune.

JUNE 16, 1920

NGS NEGROES

3 DRAGGED FROM JAIL AND HANGED AT STREET CORNE

Lynchers Will Be Prosecuted By Att'y Greene

POLICE POWERLESS IN FACE OF ANGRY CROW FIRED BY VENGEAN

Clergy's Plea of Mercy for Girl's As- sails Scorned By Executioners; T Die Proclaiming Their Innocen

4-HOUR BATTLE WAGED BY MOB TO GET VICTIMS

STREET CORN

POLICE POWERLESS
FACE OF ANGRY CRO
FIRED BY VENGEA

TRIAL *by* MOB

Just before 11 PM the Reverend William Powers, pastor at Duluth's Sacred Heart Cathedral, returned home from dinner at a parishioner's house. He had spent a pleasant evening regaling his hosts with stories and anecdotes about sports celebrities he had met. A great sports fan, the priest had once played semiprofessional baseball in his hometown of Marquette, Michigan.

Fr. Powers had quickly distinguished himself as an eloquent and powerful speaker. Thoroughly imbued with the scriptures, he also devoured the entire works of Shakespeare, and frequently laced sermons and speeches with literary quotations. Other priests maintained he was the finest speaker ever to grace the Duluth diocese. One of his favorite themes was the obligations people had toward one another. The human family, he would reason, had certain obligations, just as they had blessings. And these obligations needed to be met with love, dignity, and grace, as God had given man the sense to meet those obligations.

A robust, handsome man standing just under six feet, he still carried the husky, broad-shouldered brawn of the athlete he had been.

His physique, strength, and sense of fair play substantially contributed to the great rapport he enjoyed with young men and boys. Highly popular, Fr. Powers had made many addresses at civic luncheons and banquets, and was one of the city's best-known clergymen.

Though Sacred Heart was located in the central neighborhood of Duluth at Second Avenue West and Fourth Street, eight blocks from the jail, Fr. Powers had also heard rumors throughout the day about what might happen to the blacks. But he could not believe that Duluthians could be so enraged as to mercilessly assail the fundamental principles of law and justice.

As he reached the rectory that evening, an acquaintance was waiting. "Father, we've got big trouble. A mob is out to lynch the Negroes. They've broken into the jail already, and won't listen to anybody. Maybe you can talk some sense into them before those black fellas get killed."

Fr. Powers leaped into the ready car and the two sped down the hill toward the jail. Most activity was centering on First Street then, and when the car was stalled at Third Avenue East and First Street by the masses in the street, Fr. Powers jumped out and ran toward the Shrine Auditorium.

Meanwhile, another Duluth priest, P.J. Maloney, also arrived at the scene, and was working his way through the crowd, talking to young men, hoping to convince them to stop and go home.

Fr. Maloney was born in Dun County, Limerick, and received most of his education in Ireland. He was ordained at St. Paul's Seminary. A solid block of a man standing a shade over six feet tall and weighing 255 pounds, Fr. Maloney fit the stereotype of the Irish priest in America. Jolly, good-natured, he was also noted for his compassion. The sick and elderly found a ready listener and sympathizer in Fr. Maloney. Though not an orator of Fr. Powers's magnitude, Fr. Maloney was widely known throughout the city and in much of northern Minnesota, where he had served parishes for over thirty years.

He made no public pronouncements at the scene, but instead moved within the mob, and when he recognized a boy he knew, Fr. Maloney approached him, saying, "You've no business here, boy. Go on to your home now. This is no place for a good Catholic young fellow." Now and then one might have heeded, and the priest kept on. "This is terribly wrong, boys. In the name of God, stop it. You'll be sorry for this the rest of your lives!"

One young man, however, sneered. "Stay out of this, Father. This has nothing to do with God."

By now the quivering, battered Isaac McGhie was thrust forward toward the light pole. He stumbled, and was kicked savagely. He rolled over, his mouth open, and was snatched up. The rope was lowered over his neck. Women and young matrons cheered and laughed at the crude wit of some of the youthful onlookers who sang and joked.

"See what you are coming to."

"Now hang gracefully."

"Show us some real style."

"The less you kick, the less you'll hurt."

An intense rush of adrenaline propelled Fr. Powers, and with his sturdy hands he tossed aside several men as he scrambled toward the pole. Those holding McGhie stood back as the red-faced priest stormed forward, not merely to confront those with McGhie. Fr. Powers climbed the pole himself. The mob fell uneasily quiet, preparing to listen to the priest.

"We're wasting time!" someone hollered out, but was in turn silenced by those around him.

"Men, you don't know this man is guilty," Fr. Powers began, his voice carrying distinctly over the murmuring of the mob. Sweat glistened in his dark, curly hair, and had begun to run down his face, forming droplets on his nose and chin. "I know this crime is the most horrible one," he continued, "but let the law take its course." Some in the crowd booed, but they quieted when Powers held up his hand. "It's not too late to stop this tragedy, men. In the name of God and the church I represent, I ask you to stop."

There was a momentary silence before several men cried, "To hell with the law!"

"Lynch him!" screamed scores of others.

"Remember the girl!"

Several men near the pole reached up and pulled Fr. Powers down, but he tried to mount it again. "Men, I ask you—"

This time the priest was rudely interrupted with cries of "Lynch him! String him up! . . . The dirty black snakes!" And Fr. Powers was toppled once more and pushed back within the mob. He made one more futile attempt to reach McGhie as the young man was pulled to the pole again.

McGhie had seemed dazed moments before during Fr. Powers's attempt to save him, but he was fully conscious now. As the noose was adjusted around his neck, he shrieked, "God be with me. I'm not the right man." He was hoisted to his feet, and the rope was drawn up, but he fell when the rope loosened. A thin, short man near him tried choking McGhie, but was pulled back as the rope was refastened and McGhie was lifted up a few feet off the ground, just clear of the pavement. The crowd had pressed so close that as McGhie gasped in his death agony, blood blown from his parted lips spattered on the faces of those near him.

"String him up so we can see," demanded the mob. But the rope was too short and the body could be raised up only a few more inches.

And now a new rope was run to the pole, carried over the head of a youth in a green shirt. He was grinning and accepted the cheers of the mob. Then nineteen-year-old Elmer Jackson was dragged to the pole. One of the men near the pole wore the uniform of the U.S. Navy, and stepped forward when one in the mob called, "Let the sailor tie the knot." The sailor grinned awkwardly, then quickly fastened a noose about Jackson's neck.

Jackson, however, did not struggle. His face was calm and without emotion as he gazed at the rope taut above his head. He stared out at the mob, and as he was positioned a bit to the right of McGhie's dangling body, he drew a pair of dice from his pocket and faced the mob. "I won't need these any more in this world," he stated evenly, and threw them on the pavement.

A young man picked them up and offered them back to Jackson. "Well, you might want to roll 'em in the next," he said.

The noose was cinched about his neck, and a cluster of ready hands drew his body up. As he went into dying convulsions, the crowd began to cheer and whistle, and as he died, his body was lowered a few feet, where it hung before the howling mob.

The remaining blacks continued to be questioned in the cell. Those interrogating them, however, seemed to lose their stomachs for the affair, and several left the cell and filtered back through the still-crowded cell room and front office. Their places were taken by others eager for revenge, and the intense, but disorganized questioning went on. Two were dead. But there were four more.

TRIAL *by* MOB

11*:30 PM*—Chief Murphy's car neared the fire station, where he abandoned it after being warned by Farrell that cars belonging to police were in danger of being demolished by the mob. From Sixth Avenue West and First Street, the officers could hear the mob; they began jogging east on First Street to First Avenue West, then down to Superior Street and on to the station, where over a thousand people still clustered around the headquarters or were packed inside.

The officers tried to get in, but the crowd kept them back. "Disperse! Get out of here!" Murphy ordered. "We'll get every nigger convicted that's implicated! I promise you that!"

"Let us in!" Fiskett shouted. "We're police officers."

"Get the hell out of here, or we'll get you, too!" a man yelled at the captain.

Then, with Schulte and Murphy pushing Fiskett in as far as he could penetrate through the front door, a group within the mob turned and shoved back until the three were outside again.

"Let's get out of here, where we can get the militia," Murphy shouted, and the police managed to get inside the city hall next door. But since no phones were working, they left the building and began rounding up all police officers in the vicinity.

As they were accomplishing this, the third black, nineteen-year-old Elias Clayton, was given to the mob and brought to Second Avenue East to the same pole that held the bodies of McGhie and Jackson. Clayton's eyes widened with horror as he saw the bodies. "Please, oh God, don't kill me! I am innocent!"

Though his cries were lost as the mob jammed around the pole, they apparently had some effect on the men holding him. They paused, looked at each other, and seemed to be contemplating what they had already done. None seemed willing to make a decision, but the mob made it for them. "Lynch the third one! Lynch the third one!"

As three burly men forced Clayton through the crush of the crowd, several struck him, but the doomed man made no effort to avoid their blows. The noose was already set, and two men waited as Clayton was shoved toward them. He again pleaded for his life, but was silenced by a punch in the mouth. A knot was secured about his neck, and he was rapidly drawn up the pole, high above the mob. As he was pulled aloft, he raised his hands heavenward in a gesture of supplication before convulsing in his choking spasms. Then, like the other two, he twitched slowly, sporadically, and was still.

As he died, a man positioned high up on the pole kicked repeatedly at Clayton's face and head, and before he descended, tied the rope to one of the pole spikes so the body would remain in place. Then, nearing the ground, the man was cheered, and many clapped him on the back or shook his hand.

As the mob stood gazing at the bodies, someone yelled, "Throw a little light on the subject!" A large auto was driven toward the pole, and its searchlight was turned on Clayton, who was positioned highest on the pole. Blood still dripped from his mouth and nose, and formed great crimson smears over his bared chest. The mob stood silently for a few moments, apparently waiting to see if any others would be brought out for hanging.

Several suggested than that the photographer get some pictures. and Clayton's body was dropped to the ground to be within photographic range. A number of men formed a half-circle around the pole and the bodies, and Ralph Greenfield, a photographer from Superior, Wisconsin, took several shots while the mob patiently posed, a few smirking and joking.

"Send them pictures to Alabama," someone said. "Tell 'em to keep their niggers."

In a few days, postcards with the lynching picture were printed and quickly sold out at various retail outlets in Duluth.

After Clayton had been hanged, Maj. Beecher found Chief Murphy and explained who he was and how he felt the situation should be handled. The chief agreed, and assigned twelve men to the major and told them to take orders from Beecher. Then Murphy directed other officers to start throwing out the few stragglers who remained in the demolished station.

Beecher and his men found rifles of U.S. Model 1873 caliber .45-70 Springfields with fixed bayonets and issued them to men on duty. He then ordered the men to form a line around the station on Second Avenue East and ordered them to permit no forming into crowds. With other officers, Beecher ran down Superior Street to First Avenue East, breaking up all gatherings and moving people away from the station.

As the crowds dispersed at the sight of armed police, Beecher made another call to Gen. Rhinow. The major was instructed to call out the home guards and get in touch with the commanding officer of the tank company, and to order that unit on immediate duty. Beecher called

Capt. Moerke before going home to change into his military uniform.

The major was not surprised at the ease with which the mob was broken up. In his own mind, he felt that twenty-five men prepared to use weapons could have easily prevented violence and saved the lives of the three victims.

The chief, in the meantime, took a badly dented police car and spirited the three remaining prisoners across the bay to Superior, where they would spend the rest of the night in that city's jail.

12:30 AM, Wednesday, June 16, 1920—Capt. Moerke, having just received mobilization orders, was able to order his men to immediate duty because he had the foresight to tell the troops to stand by. Within minutes, 104 men converged on the downtown streets, though by now there was little to do except chase loiterers.

Minnesota Governor J.A.A. Burnquist had been delivering a commencement address at his alma mater, Carleton College in Northfield, the night of June 15. He had graduated with honors there in 1902. The governor had been first elected to the state's House of Representatives in 1908, then was elected lieutenant governor as a Republican in 1914, assuming the governor's office in 1915 upon the death of Democratic governor Winfield S. Hammond.

A popular official, Burnquist won reelection in 1915 and 1918. Ironically, since 1916, he also served as president of the St. Paul branch of the National Association for the Advancement of Colored People.

Upon notification of the lynchings in Duluth, Burnquist arranged to dispatch troops to that city about 1:30 AM, and ordered a train held in St. Paul for troop movement.

By two-thirty 124 men and six officers equipped for riot duty, in addition to a four-man medical unit, lined up on Sibley Street in St. Paul in the bleak dark and boarded Northern Pacific train Number 66 to Duluth. The train had added two special coaches to accommodate the men and their accompanying ammunition. There were seven thousand rounds of ball rifle ammunition and two thousand rounds of pistol cartridges.

By that time, too, mopping-up operations were well under way in downtown Duluth, headed by thirty-five police officers. They arrived on the scene near the Shrine Auditorium and ran off about a hundred onlookers, while the bodies of Jackson and McGhie twisted in the wind. The hangmen's ropes creaked over the steel pole—the only sound except for the scraping of paper blowing over concrete. The bodies were carefully, almost reverently, cut down, as though officers felt they were, perhaps, making up for their dereliction of duty earlier by treating corpses with respect.

The bodies were removed to the Grady and Horgan Funeral Parlor for examination and processing, but under anonymous threats that company deferred, and the bodies were eventually sent to the Crawford Mortuary.

Further patrolling of downtown streets continued with the added force of the tank company; by 2:45 AM, peace had returned.

An uneasy quiet covered the homes of Duluth blacks, most of whom were aware that lynchings had occurred. Rumors had spread throughout the scattered black community that all Duluth blacks might be lynched. And when the doorbell rang at 619 North Fifth Street at 2:05 AM, it carried a jolt, breaking the funereal silence. Eddie Nichols almost panicked and leaped to his feet. The bell sounded again, and Rodney and his wife looked at Nichols. The young man reached for his pistol and cocked it. He pulled on an ankle-length overcoat, keeping the loaded weapon in his right hand under the coat. As the bell repeated a third time, Nichols took a deep breath, felt his sweating, trembling fingers tense around the trigger, and tip-toed to the door. He cracked it open several inches, and slid the pistol forward. He was ready to fire.

On the steps outside stood a lone white man, who stepped back when the door opened. "T-telegram for Mr. Rodney," he stammered, thrusting a yellow paper through the door.

Nichols breathed deeply and exhaled. "You don't know how close you came to being a dead man," he coldly announced to the messenger. Without a word the deliverer backed off the porch and fled.

The telegram was from the state militia offering full protection for Duluth blacks, and asking if the Rodney house might be maintained as Guard headquarters. While the household welcomed protection, Rodney sensed that the days ahead would be trying ones for the city's blacks, and he was not prepared to let whites into his house. He refused the request.

Most Duluth blacks agreed with his decision. If the strength of the mob which had grown to include nearly one-tenth of the local population could so easily overpower police, what would happen to the relatively isolated blacks once the National Guard pulled out, as it surely would? Days might be bleak, indeed, for any Duluth black who harbored the militia in his house.

During the three days following the lynchings, while many Duluthians still debated the pros and cons of the crimes, a nation was reacting to the horror of June 15. The renowned poet James Weldon Johnson, in his capacity as field secretary of the NAACP, sent a telegram to Gov. Burnquist the morning of June 16:

The National Association for the Advancement of Colored People offers all possible assistance in apprehending murderers who battered down door of jail at Duluth last night and lynched three Negroes accused of connections with attack on girl. Prompt apprehension and rigorous punishment of lynchers of Negroes and of the law of the state of Minnesota will have wholesome and salutary effect throughout nation. As governor of state and president of St. Paul branch of NAACP may we urge you use every power at your command to prevent further disorder and arrest lynchers. Commend action in sending troops. Advise us if we can be of assistance. Can furnish investigator if needed.

Although Gov. Burnquist did not request an investigator from the national office, the St. Paul branch, through local attorney William Francis, hired the Employer's Detective Service to mount a private investigation into the lynchings and the events leading up to them. The subsequent investigation would uncover a number of pertinent points that for unexplained reasons never found their way into court. Perhaps lack of communications played a role here, or, as has been implied, petty jealousies arose among lawyers hired to defend blacks accused of raping Sandra Teale.

Within the week, most major newspapers in the country had editorialized concerning the lynchings. Duluth's *News Tribune* comments were directed at the lack of police fortitude. "It was a case where the right man was not there. Few would have dared face a gun held by a man who meant business. No one would have acted, save mob support."

"Duluth has now joined the American cities which have discovered how easily the safeguards of civilized justice can be leaped," observed the June 17 *Chicago Tribune.* "In the Duluth lynching, motives of sex protection and race instinct were combined ... All America has in this new lynching a cause for gravest reflection. The mob heard appeals to let the law take its course. Its members did not heed those appeals because they themselves wanted to kill."

The *New York World* noted, "Like every other town similarly situated, Duluth's repentance will hardly be considered genuine unless its public opinion is powerful enough to inflict upon every recreant officer the prescribed penalty for his shameful betrayal of duty."

And the June 19 edition of the *The New York Times* held that " ... No valid or even colorable claim in behalf of Duluth can be based on the fact that three of the six Negroes were spared by the executors of 'wild justice.' In that city and state there can be no pretense that the white population is under any general menace from a black majority,.." The editorial further commented that mob violence is never justifiable and is always disgraceful to those who participate in it and to those who permit it.

But editorial writers from the other newspapers were not in Duluth that night; they had not experienced the tension and the mob. They wrote from comfortable chairs hundreds of miles away. Many Duluthians still disagreed with mounting criticism of local police. "What should the cops have done?" people asked. "Fired right into their own kind?"

That question had been somewhat answered earlier in the year when the Kentucky National Guard, protecting William Lockett, a black and self-confessed slayer of Geneva Mardigan, a ten-year-old white girl, fired on a mob that stormed the Lexington courthouse to lynch him. Four whites in that mob had been killed. But the National Guard prevailed because its officers were determined to carry out their obligations.

Few newspapers, however, took a hard look at the alleged crime that precipitated the lynchings. Among them, only one, a short-lived muckraking local weekly, the *Duluth Ripsaw,* raised a disturbing question in its June nineteenth edition. "What puzzles thinking and sophisticated people is the allegation that a tender young girl was raped six times by six big burly negroes and then was able to ride home in a streetcar and said nothing to her parents about her terrible treatment."

That racial hatred figured prominently in the crime was the focus of an editorial entitled "The Duluth Disgrace" in the *Minneapolis Journal* on June 17. The paper stated: "It was the color of the three prisoners that made them victims of the mob. Had they been white, they might have been the objects of reprobation for the crime for which they were charged, but would no doubt have been left to the processes of the law."

Though scores of papers nationally expressed concern over the flouting of the law, lynchers were not without editorial support, at least in Minnesota. The June 16 headline in the *Mankato* (Minnesota) *Daily Free Press,* for instance, emblazoned: BLACK HAWKS SWUNG FROM POLE. The following day, this paper editorialized in a column entitled "The Duluth Tragedy":

The people of Duluth appear to express a greater amount of indignation over the lynching of three negroes in that city than they do over the terrible outrage that caused the stringing up of the black fiends. The city of Duluth is not disgraced. There have been other lynchings in other cities and towns survived. Lynch law is to be deplored. But the crime which led up to the rule of the mob is more deplorable . . . And it must be understood that white men—men of blood—will not sit idly by when black rascals pounce like fiends on white women . . . In such instances the anger of the mob knows no restraint. They are out to avenge foul deeds. Mad dogs are shot dead without ceremony. Beasts in human shape are entitled to but scant consideration . . .

The *Ely Miner,* an Iron Range weekly, also showed strong mob sympathies in its June 18 editorial:

The happenings in Duluth on Tuesday when three negroes were made victims of lynch law, is to be regretted by all lovers of law and order. The crime for which the men were lynched was one of the most fiendish ever perpetrated in this county, and we have had some bad ones. Those who gathered to mete out justice did so without the added impetus of the skin full of booze. The consensus of opinion throughout the county is that while the thing was wrong in principle, it is most effective and those who were put out of their criminal existence by the mob will not assault any more young girls. The mob is not as bloodthirsty as may be imagined—had they been such, and had the race hatred spoken predominated, the other three held in jail would have met a like fate . . . As we said before, the lynching is to be deplored. There were fathers, brothers, husbands, sons concerned in the affair. Suppose it was your daughter, sister, wife or mother—what would you do?

The next week, in a follow-up item, the *Miner* observed—"The lynching in Duluth will have a wholesome effect on the class of help carried by ordinary circus and carnival troupes. The chances are that no colored help with a carnival attraction or circus in the county will be tolerated hereafter."

In the aftermath of criticism, most Duluthians assumed an impassive posture toward the lynchings, feeling it was best not to discuss it further. This was not an attitude sustained by some city clergymen, causing no little consternation within various congregations. Ministers like Dr. George Brewer, pastor of the First Presbyterian Church, believed that the pulpit must serve as a public conscience, reminding people that not only was the lynching contrary to man's law, but violated the higher law of God as well.

A native of Kingston, Ontario, Dr. Brewer had lived in the United States for thirty years, and received his education at Princeton Theological Seminary. He had served the Duluth congregation since 1916. At the time of the lynching, Dr. Brewer was in the process of terminating his service in Duluth, and preparing to move to Grosse Pointe, Michigan.

The lynching supplied the text for one of his sermons the following Sunday. "Why This Crime, and Why These Lynchings?" was the title of a widely reprinted message in which Dr. Brewer asserted that white Americans were largely to blame for the substandard plight of blacks.

On June 16, he was quoted in the *News Tribune*—"I am appalled at the situation Duluth finds herself in today. She is humiliated among law-abiding, order-loving cities of our land. No defense can be made for the work of this mob."

A Duluth priest, the Rev, O.W. Ryan, said, "We are all humiliated by the disgraceful violence of the mob . . . We feel the police failed lamentably in their duty. It is not good policy for guardians of the public to shoot in general, but here was plenty of warning; here was the dignity of the law to be upheld; here was the opportunity to quell any unrestraining violence which might break forth at any time."

Even as the city's clergy reminded Duluthians that a horrible wrong had been committed, and those involved as participants or bystanders had erred with enormity, the business of returning the city to normal continued.

National Guardsmen patrolled black neighborhoods, and civic leaders mapped other strategies for coping with potential future outbreaks. A communique was issued by St. Louis attorney Greene's office, declaring that none of the blacks involved in the assault was from the city. Greene hoped this might quiet rising animosities among whites who now viewed blacks with open fear and hatred.

TRIAL *by* MOB

7*:30 AM*—Troops from Company H from Faribault, and Company I from Long Prairie, arrived at the downtown Duluth railroad station as the city began coming to life. It was a slow, thick awakening after a nightmare. The downtown streets were quiet, though debris and litter clogged curbside gutters and sewers.

Maj. Beecher, who had met the train, conferred with Gen. Rhinow, and escorted troops to Superior Street and over to the shambles that had been the police station. Almost every window was smashed, and water still ran over the front sidewalk; the whistling of wind through the paneless windows of the station gave a ghostlike quality to the nearly deserted street.

Inside the jail were hammers and iron pinchers, remains of the attack. Stuck fast in a bar of a cell door was a first-class machinist's saw blade. The walls, inside and out, were pocked, and loose plaster and chips of paint had clumped together in moist heaps on the floor. Far over the gaping windows of the demolished station, the American flag fluttered gently in the morning breeze.

THURSDAY MORNING

GUARDS SENT HERE TO KEEP ORDER

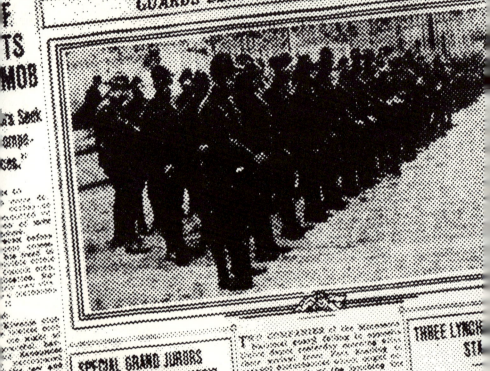

SPECIAL GRAND JURORS WHO WILL PROBE MOB'S LYNCHING OF NEGROES

EXPECTS SUPPORT OF PROGRESSIVES

Senator McTaggart Wires Harding His First Republican Presidential Choice.

THREE LYNCH

CAPTAIN'S

PRIVAT

The militia swung into precise action, mapping out areas of the city where blacks lived, and two guardsmen were dispatched to patrol every block.

Gen. Rhinow met with Sheriff Magie, who had meanwhile deputized several hundred local citizens who had been outraged by the lynchings. These men had been assigned to guard the county jail.

By 8:15 AM many Duluthians on their way to work paused to look at the station, then walked to the lynch site. Many may have hoped for souvenirs, and some picked scraps of broken glass or splinters of wood from in front of the station. Outside the Shrine Auditorium, it was pointed out to thousands where the bodies had fallen, and that the rope had been thrown there.

Troops moved the curious farther back from both the lynch site and the police station, and citizens did not argue with the armed soldiers.

A small naval unit was also placed under Gen. Rhinow's command, and it conducted an impressive weapons demonstration that evening, revealing strength that would discourage the foolhardy. But rumors of more attacks and lynchings continued throughout the day in Duluth. And black families still received anonymous threats by early-morning phone calls and predawn bricks thrown through windows.

By nine Gen. Rhinow headed out with several truckloads of Guardsmen to a remote spot on Vermilion Road where he met two heavily-armed automobile parties who had kept guard throughout the night over the four blacks brought from Virginia by car. Quietly, these blacks were brought into town, and a quick run was made to the county jail. Few residents were aware of this transfer. Then a similar run was made from Superior with the three blacks the mob had left in the city jail the night before. And under heavy guard, the six blacks who had come down from Virginia by train during the early morning were likewise sequestered in the county jail.

Gen. Rhinow, taking no chances, stationed nineteen Guardsmen in the cells with the thirteen blacks, and Maj. Beecher issued a statement to the local press—"No one will get any more Negroes until the last soldier has been killed and many of the rioters. I have given orders to shoot to kill."

The large banner headline in the morning *News Tribune* blared: DULUTH MOB HANGS NEGROES, and beneath it ran reporter A.J. Carson's copious and thorough account of about 7500 words.

Carson, who was downtown as the mob was forming, remained at the scene throughout the night, rushing between the lynch site and the jail, where questioning of blacks continued during the hangings. Carson was apparently given cooperation by many in the mob, and consequently managed to compile the data on the tragedy, under the most difficult of circumstances, with only a few minor errors.

Official Duluth reaction was predictably sober. Mayor Magney deplored the stain on the city, and Sheriff Magie was inundated with requests from men wishing to be deputized. The American Legion, smarting because several of its members were apparently involved in the crimes, offered two thousand men to be deployed under Ed McDevitt's command to maintain order on the streets while the police department regrouped.

St. Louis County Attorney Warren E. Greene stated that those connected with the lynchings would be firmly prosecuted. "The original crime was one of the most atrocious ever committed in this county," Greene told the *Tribune.* "But neither this nor any other crime justifies the resorting to mob law."

But the lynchings and the alleged precipitating crime would prove fitful and distressing for Greene. A strikingly handsome man of forty-five, with blond wavy hair and an aquiline nose, Greene had been county attorney for seven years. He was considered to be a man ready for wider political accomplishments. During the April primary election, he finished a strong third behind Judges Cant and Fesler for a seat on the district bench, outpolling Mayor Magney by nearly two thousand votes. Three judges would be elected to serve, and Greene appeared to have the inside track for that third position.

His looks could be counted on to get votes from the newly franchised women, but beyond this he had maintained a proud record as county attorney. He was duty-bound to prosecute lynchers and rioters whose actions probably had received at least tacit approval from most of the county's residents. True, there would be cases brought against the blacks for the assault, but that they would be convicted was almost a foregone conclusion. Going after rioters and murderers would prove sticky. Arrests would doubtless be made, but would convictions logically follow? And would vigorous prosecution hurt Greene's future ambition?

J.A.O. Preuss, the Republican candidate for governor in place of Burnquist, who had decided to retire, had scheduled June 16 as a day for campaigning in Duluth. During his speech he utilized the occasion to state that he favored strict law for assaults on women. "If I am elected governor, I will do all in my power to increase the penalty," he said. "I will sign any bill the legislature will pass along this line, and I'm in favor of making the penalty as severe as possible."

As the day progressed, thousands visited the station and lynch site, but the curious were cautious, and kept their distance. They spoke in hushed voices under the scrutiny of troops and special deputies.

Stories circulated throughout town and appeared in city newspapers praising Lt. Barber for his role in attempting to prevent lynchings, and also commending the order not to use firearms, which the press assumed came from Barber. Barber also won the respect of Duluth blacks who felt he had at least tried to see justice prevail. Public reaction to Barber's role at first seemed favorable, and those reactions displeased Murnian. He called in a reporter and hotly denounced the stories generated by the paper, stressing that he should have been given credit for the order not to shoot. "I gave strict orders to all men to use firearms under no consideration, and I believe this had a great deal to do with the lack of serious injuries," he stated for publication.

But criticism of police handling of the affair, and of Murnian, mounted during the next twenty-four hours, and the commissioner was forced to issue yet another statement to the press—"The force was not large enough to handle such a situation, and by the time we could get all the available police in the city and the Sheriff's force assembled, the crowd had gone beyond the control of any force many times larger than at our disposal. Despite criticism, I still believe I was right in ordering police not to shoot, for if they had shot into the crowd and killed one woman or child, the criticism and condemnation of the department would have been more severe."

If the lynchings left Duluth stunned, no less shocked was the neighboring city of Superior, Wisconsin, where the "knee-jerk" reaction of Acting Police Chief Louis Osborne drew praise. "We're going to run all idle Negroes out of Superior, and they're going to stay out," Osborne said.

Larry Boyd, manager of a carnival in Superior, dismissed all black employees, saying, "I shall never hire another one, even though I have never as yet had any trouble with them."

The decision of both men triggered another brief panic in Duluth. Most blacks forced out of Superior left on foot, and nervous Duluth whites flooded Magie's office with calls reporting hundreds of blacks coming from Superior to join up with Duluth blacks to kill the whites. Duluth police, again put on alert, did stop several blacks, ignorant of the lynchings the night before, trying to find sanctuary in Duluth.

As anger and criticism of police seemed to be overwhelming early police support, the department issued statements from time to time, assuring citizens that the lynched men had all been implicated by other witnesses and, in fact, no "innocent" men had died.

Duluth blacks, frustrated, frightened, and isolated, felt total despair. There was no NAACP to calm their fears or to give needed moral support during the crisis. Black children were mostly kept indoors by parents, and those youngsters who did get out to play, were subjected to name-calling and abuse previously unknown to them in that city.

Franklin Cox, the only black of school age in the fashionable Lester Park neighborhood of Duluth, was twelve years old then, and regarded himself as tough and able to handle most encounters. But for weeks after the lynchings, he feared going out of the house, especially after dark. Gangs of bigger white boys constantly taunted him and picked fights. Franklin, however, became toughened by the hassles, and engaged white youths in the intimacy of fists, eventually gaining a grudging respect. But years would pass before he could ever again feel moderately at ease in the presence of whites.

MILIE BUNNELL
MANAGER

EDITORIAL

Devoted to Public Service: In City, State and Nation

DULUTH'S Disgrace.

TRIAL *by* MOB

On June 17, District Court Judge W.A. Cant convened the grand jury. This grand jury was typical, comprised of men with substantial influence within the community—businessmen, bankers, men of financial status, religious laymen, members of country clubs. They represented families and organizations for whom blacks had toiled for years as domestics. Most of all, they were friends of Judge Cant, whose philosophy was decidedly conservative.

Aware of the spotlight attention, the judge read a statement over which he'd labored for nearly twelve hours. His glasses resting loosely far down the bridge of his nose, he read in a strong voice, reminiscent of a fervent evangelist:

The awful scenes enacted in this city within the past forty-eight hours have necessitated the convening of your body in extraordinary session at this time. The most atrocious crime in all our history has been committed in the open defiance of authority, in disregard of law and attended by horrors such as will ineffaceably scar the minds and conscience of us all.

That the victims may have committed another crime also hei-

nous, is not the slightest excuse. Indeed, that is beside the question. They were in the custody of officers and behind barred doors. They were entitled to the protection of the law. There was not the least danger that they would escape trial and punishment. The bars that kept them in were equally designed to keep all others out.

The great wrong to the victims wholly beyond our power of estimation can never be undone. The laws of God and man have been defiled, set at naught. In our midst from this time forth, the laws of God will be held less sacred, life will be less safe, property less secure, and humanity itself of every character will be held more cheap. Instead of progressing constantly forward, we have taken a long step backward.

Viewed either locally or nationwide, human progress is made possible only in safeguarding those rules designed for the control of human conduct, which have been crystalized into law. Those laws are often imperfect . . . but at any particular period . . . human rights are preserved and protected and vindicated, only through a faithful and conscientious observance and strict enforcement of the law, whatever it may be.

The violence of the mob spirit of perhaps very few men and the encouragement of others who should have been on the side of right rather than great wrong, has brought about a condition with which you have to deal. Do not proceed in a bitter and vindictive spirit. But with righteous indignation, which, if possible, will reach all who had to do with the deplorable incident. Let everyone know that notwithstanding those incidents, we have a citizenship which denounces such outrages and which will do its utmost to discover and punish the perpetrators thereof.

By the afternoon of the seventeenth, Gov. Burnquist's office had been flooded with telegrams and letters from private citizens as well as numerous black organizations.

Maude Craig, secretary of the Universal Negro Improvement Association, wrote: "We hereby beseech your honor to keep the good old state of Minnesota from falling to the degraded level of that state of Georgia, or any other heathen vicinity, by putting forth strenuous efforts to bring the murderous perpetrators of that terrible deed face to face with the awful justice it deserves."

Another telegram from James Weldon Johnson requested Gov. Burnquist to exert more influence in undertaking an immediate investigation in Duluth. But Burnquist would not order an inquiry, believing the problem properly belonged to Duluth, where it should be handled without meddling by down-state politicians. Instead, he asked Gen. Rhinow to examine the police structure in Duluth, to determine why discipline broke down, and how the mob could meet with so little resistance.

The investigation urged by Johnson was independently undertaken by the Employer's Detective Service, and an agent known only as Morgan set out for Duluth from St. Paul on June 16.

Thirteen blacks were eventually brought to the St. Louis County jail in Duluth. They were Nathan Green, Loney Williams, John Thomas, Charles Harris, Albert Small, Early Thomas, William Miller, Clarence Green, Max Mason, Louis Hays, Frank Spicer, Eugene Jefferson, and Normal Ausley.

And despite the furor over the lynchings, police and sheriff's deputies had spent several hours the night of the sixteenth, and on the following day, trying to obtain confessions or at least testimonies that might implicate some prisoners in the assault on Sandra Teale. But the thirteen remained firm, denying guilt and failing to implicate anyone. Police speculated that the prisoners were either incredibly stubborn, or in the words of one city patrolman, "almost void of intelligence."

Warren Greene, too, had hoped for confessions which would have doubtless blunted negative reactions when the grand jury indicted leaders of the mob.

The two days following the assault and lynchings saw Duluth blacks—already close-knit—become closer and more militant. The fierce loyalty that had previously seen blacks lend support to a neighbor's family when a job was lost, or when illness or death struck, turned into a more desperate need—protection. But many blacks began leaving the city. In the months ahead, about two hundred blacks would depart Duluth.

As rumors continued circulating among whites that blacks from Gary were arming and preparing to take open revenge on whites, young blacks like Eddie Nichols, who were emerging as leaders, denied the rumors, but emphasized they would aggressively protect themselves from any roving bands of whites bent on further violence.

But the city stayed at least superficially calm. Soldiers and special deputies found little to do, except to check out potentially explosive rumors—all of which proved groundless.

By the morning of Friday, June 18, Gen. Rhinow ordered Companies H and I back to Camp Rosenwald at Fort Snelling. This order upset Sheriff Magie, who anticipated troops in the city at least through the weekend. If a number of West Duluth men got hold of liquor, Magie reasoned, things might start all over again. "They'll be armed this time," he told Gen. Rhinow, "and if there's been drinking, there could be a real bloodbath."

But Rhinow's order stayed, and even as troops were lining up at the Michigan Street railway station for the trip back to St. Paul, Magie received threatening phone calls.

"No soldier boys to save the niggers now, Sheriff," said one. "If you don't want your jail destroyed, clear out by five o'clock tonight," warned another.

Magie relayed these messages to Rhinow who reversed his earlier order. Though breathing more easily, Magie requested even more troops, hoping to show the locals that once and for all those in authority meant business.

Maj. Beecher, reacting angrily to the phone threats, told the *News Tribune*, "The orders are to shoot and guards will carry out those orders."

Magie increased the guard around the jail, and drew a line around the compound about twenty feet from the building. In the presence of a hundred sullen men who were watching troops guard the jail, Magie shouted, "There will be no more rioting or attempts to take prisoners from the county jail without serious consequences." He pointed to the soldiers who still carried weapons with fixed bayonets.

At six that evening, another anonymous call was received, stating a group would be storming the jail on Saturday, and advising deputies and troops to clear out.

Gen. Rhinow, hearing about the threat from the harried sheriff, ordered in more soldiers; by 8 AM on the nineteenth, another 101 men arrived with four machine guns and several thousand rounds of ammunition.

Saturday evening, June 19, 1920—Far into the night, lights burned inside the county jail as deputies and troops peered into the darkness outside, illumined only by the glowing tips of cigarettes the guards outside were smoking. Inside, men smoked and talked quietly, though on occasion a brief laugh erupted, cracking the rigid tension. Near the cells, jailers paced, drank coffee, stared at the clock. Nine o'clock—ten—ten-thirty.

The strain of the past week wore on their faces. On a normal night, if you were on the sheriff's staff, you'd have been heading home at midnight. Now you were on emergency duty until further notice. You didn't feel the blacks were worth this kind of attention, and may have thought that if only the mob had gotten the rest of them, things would have settled down, and your own life would have been less fraught with anxieties. You could have promised your wife you'd be home as usual, and eat regular meals again, and sleep regular hours. The drinking of coffee by the countless cups, the smoking of dry cigarettes, did not set well with the stomach, and you always went home finally about dawn, with jumpy nerves and a mouth tasting stale.

And what was it the neighbor said the other day? "Why all the fuss? They was just niggers."

But this night, like last night and the night before, would be endured. The worst thing was the waiting. If only something had happened. Something besides those damned phone calls which warned you to watch yourself, to be careful, or to leave the "niggers."

It was times like these, you told yourself, if you were a deputy or a cop, bringing home that skimpy $115-$125 each month, that you wished you had taken that nice safe railroad job, or had gone up north cutting timber. That was fit enough work for a man, and God knows, you were big enough and strong enough. But thinking about it did no good. And you knew it, and couldn't help yourself. And as you thought about how bad it was on your system, you helped yourself to yet another cup of coffee, lit another cigarette, and watched the clock. And waited.

TRIAL *by* MOB

11*:45 PM, Saturday, June 19, 1920*—Word came back to the jail that there didn't seem to be any groups forming anywhere in the city. The patrols had been out all over; armored trucks lumbered through the West End and West Duluth. There were some mean stares from folks, but no backtalk, no trouble. By now the undercover boys were filtering back, too—troops in civilian clothes who'd been mingling with local citizens; they reported nothing unusual.

Midnight—"I think the worst of it is over," a soldier told Beecher and Magie. "The people don't have no stomach for it no more."

Inside the cell room, some of the blacks tried to sleep under the muted glare of the lights in the halls. One anguished prisoner whispered to his guard, "They coming tonight, mister man?"

"Nobody's coming to get you out of here, boy," the guard replied, and the black nodded his thanks. "I hope not," he said. "Lord, I do hope not."

Sunday, June 20, 1920—Another day and night of waiting passed. But this time the card games in the jail and in the backs of trucks were good-natured. The spirit of the mob had been broken. Even the coffee seemed to taste fresher, and provided welcome breaks now instead of extending the monotony and tension.

A corporal read a psalm from his Bible and offered a quiet prayer of thanks for the peace of another day, and for the absence of further violence.

Troops and special deputies made plans to return home, to enter fresh-made beds and feel cool, clean linen against tired, aching limbs.

If you were an ordinary officer or deputy, or even one sworn in for special duty during the disruptions, you were able to count on going home, your job completed. That justice had been denied three men was a fact. It was too bad, but the daily routine, after all, beckoned, and, for sure, such a thing could never happen again. There'd be stories to tell among the neighbors who'd ask all sorts of questions, and if you were on duty, you could discuss it all now, and you could comment on how it was, and how the newspapers always got things screwed up. You'd say nothing about how it was mostly waiting around and chewing the rag. Sure, you probably agreed with Murnian that no white man should have risked his life for a black. Still, they could have been tried, like they were supposed to have been. They'd have all rotted in their cells at Stillwater State Prison anyway. And besides, that girl was probably fooling around with her boyfriend at the circus. You had heard the talk. And you knew, too, that many Duluth blacks figured the girl was just a prostitute on the prowl. Well, you didn't go quite that far yourself, but probably thought the "niggers" just wanted in on a little action. But most of all, you were tired. Very tired.

TRIAL *by* MOB

Detective Morgan from the Employer's Detective Service was a listener, an eavesdropper, a penetrating observer with an eye for detail, and ear for innuendo. And on his visit to Duluth, he kept his senses honed on the periphery of local gossip as he diligently probed for background data. He might have expected difficulties bringing his investigation into the open on a case of this sort; at first, he found many folks unwilling to discuss it. The Walsh family refused to talk to him. But he did land a break.

Sandra Teale agreed to see him if her mother could be present. And Dr. Graham said he would see Morgan. Morgan also checked in with Murphy and Sheriff Magie, and both men said they had no reason to believe the girl was not of good character.

As Morgan began his examination into the alleged rape, he wanted to get medical opinion from doctors without appearing obvious. He selected the Lyceum Drug Store on the corner of Fifth Avenue West and Superior Street, where a number of doctors made regular stops. He did not engage a doctor in conversation there, but found a willing talker in Albert Busch, a clerk. "Well, I heard doctors saying here all week that Graham wasn't sure the girl had been raped," Busch said. "From what I hear, this Walsh was taking liberties with her at the time the Negroes were supposed to have assaulted her. Lots of folks say the boy isn't the decent sort. Mr. Blodgett sure hasn't got nothing good to say about the boy."

Blodgett owned a shoestore at Seventh Avenue West. He told Morgan he knew Walsh, but wished he didn't. "A wild, vicious character that nearly a year ago, with a party of young men and girls, broke into my summer cottage on Lake Superior. They smashed furniture, tore up bedlinen, and they had been drinking, too."

A neighboring businessman, George Hargrave, told Morgan that Walsh was a young man of evil repute. He'd drink liquor whenever he got a chance. Further, it was Hargrave's impression that the girl had been running around with men, and might have been of loose morals.

Morgan, acting on another tip, visited the law firm of Williams and Pearson at 311 Lonsdale Building on Superior Street, where he was told again that Walsh was a woman-chaser and inclined to drink heavily.

On June 18, Morgan arrived for his appointment with the Teale family. He began by reviewing information that had already appeared in the papers. Then Sandra told him she left her house on June 14 with Bobby, though the newspaper version indicated she left alone, meeting Bobby later. Morgan did not press for clarification. She later said they met friends there and walked around for about thirty minutes. Morgan then started probing the basic issue. "How many Negroes grabbed you?"

"Four," she said.

"Did you make any attempt to cry out?"

"I did, but one of the Negroes put his hand in my mouth."

"Didn't Bobby help you?"

"He couldn't, as one of the Negroes pinned his arms and another held the gun to his head."

"How did they take hold of you?"

"They grabbed my arms and shoulders."

"What did they do then?""

"I don't know. Walsh later told me that four Negroes were fighting on top of me."

"Did you feel any ill effects after the assault?"

"Yes, my arms were a little sore."

Morgan must have been at least mildly surprised at the easy responses from the girl. She did not appear unduly distressed over her alleged encounter. "Well," he went on, "how long was it after you fainted that you came to your senses and knew what was going on?"

"I don't know. But I don't think it was very long."

"Where were the Negroes upon your regaining your senses?"

"Walking away from the place."

"Now, didn't you tell other parties in Duluth which way the Negroes directed you to leave the grounds after the assault?"

"Yes, they did direct us out."

"What did you do then?"

"Took a streetcar home and sat on the porch with Walsh about half an hour, talking about the occurrence and then went to bed."

Morgan didn't believe her, but showed no emotion, and posed the next question. "Why didn't you and Walsh, immediately after the affair, go and report it?"

"I thought it best to keep it quiet," she replied.

"Well, how did Walsh come to speak about the matter?"

"He went to work at twelve o'clock midnight, where he spots boats on the Duluth Missabe and Northern Ore Docks, and his father is night superintendent. He spoke to his father about it, and Mr. Walsh telephoned my father and they notified the police. Then they went to the circus train with Bobby. He couldn't identify any of the Negroes so they came up to our house and got me down there to identify them. They arrested twelve."

"How could you identify them more than Walsh if you fainted immediately after they grabbed you?"

"I couldn't recognize them by their faces, but only by their size and physique."

"Isn't it funny you could see more than Bobby?"

"Well, they had me about fifteen feet from where they had him."

Her almost blase responses must have struck Morgan as at least somewhat improbable. Here before him sat a girl allegedly attacked most cruelly, and yet four days later appeared outwardly calm and relaxed.

"Was any of your clothing torn?" Morgan asked.

Sandra did not respond immediately, but her mother said, "One of her garments was torn a little." The garment, a union suit, had two small tears.

"Did you have any ill effects after the assault?"

"She suffered a nervous breakdown," Mrs. Teale said.

It was time to explore the inconsistencies, Morgan believed, but such delving would prove difficult. "This nervous breakdown—that was from the notoriety that the newspapers gave the case, wasn't it?"

"Yes—I guess so."

"Now, you mentioned some boys and girls who were with you at the circus grounds. Who were they? You said at first you knew them for years. What were their names?"

"Well, I just knew them by their faces and I don't know their names."

Morgan let this pass. There would doubtless be other flaws,

and more significant ones. But before he had the opportunity to ask another question, Mrs. Teale terminated the interview. "My daughter is not well," she said. "She needs rest more than anything else."

Though annoyed at not being able to nail down concrete evidence, Morgan called Dr. Graham and asked if there were any signs of assault on the girl.

"I don't think she was raped," the doctor said.

"The girl said her arms were a little sore."

"Still, I don't think she was assaulted."

"Well, Doctor, you take a young girl like Miss Teale, and have four Negroes rape her, there would be signs of abuse, would there not?" Morgan asked.

"You would think so," said Dr. Graham.

Morgan completed his investigation the next day, but turned up little of value for his report. He returned to St. Paul on the evening train, and filed his typewritten data of twelve pages with W.J. Carling, manager of the detective agency. Carling forwarded the report to William Francis, who in turn passed it on to Gov. Burnquist. The governor, however, maintained a hands-off policy in the matter, and merely filed the report, where it remains in a folder among the archives of the State of Minnesota Historical Society. Despite the governor's affiliation with the NAACP, nowhere is there evidence to suggest that attorneys for blacks incarcerated in Duluth ever saw Morgan's report. Neither the interview with Sandra Teale nor Dr. Graham was ever introduced as evidence in the subsequent trials, nor did attorneys even ask disturbing questions such as those posed by Morgan.

In the following days, furor over the lynchings died down, but the thirteen blacks languished in the county jail. However, indictments for murder and rioting continued dotting the pages of both Duluth newspapers.

The Duluth

DULUTH, MINN., THUR

ROUNDUP OF LYNC

Police Quiz Demanded By Club;

WOOD TOO BIG FOR CONVENTION GALLANT LOSER

Political Expert Lauds General as Most Commanding Figure, Even in Defeat.

Says He Was Too Far Outside "Big Guard Circle" to Achieve Nomination.

Save State From Nonparty, Is Plea

PREUS' PLEA TO SAVE STATE IS ACCLAIMED HERE

Republicans Acclaim Candidate for Governor and Lauds Collins, His Running Mate.

Menace of Townleyism Graphically Pictured; Preus Urges State Anti-Lynch Law.

...ws Tribune.

Society Page 7

...NING, JUNE 17, 1920.

...RS STARTS TODAY

...es Order Grand Jury Investigatio...

AFTERMATH OF LYNCHING ORGY

Rumors of Renewal of Lawlessness Prove False. Girl to Confront Negro Suspects Today.

OFFICIALS WILL ACT AFTER QU... OF MOB LEADE...

SUPERIOR POLICE TO DEPORT IDLE NEGROES AT ONCE

Acting Chief [illegible] Issues Order. Carnival Discharges Plantation Show Employes.

MILITIAMEN KEPT ON DUTY TO HELP MAINTAIN ORDER

Two Companies of State Militia, Naval Militia and Tank Corps Patrol City.

On July 3, Clifford Jackson, father of Elmer Jackson, the second person of the three to be lynched, filed a suit against Duluth police for negligence, and sought $7,500 in damages. But a city attorney, John E. Samuelson, offhandedly dismissed the suit, stating, "This city is not liable." On the advice of an attorney, the elder Jackson did not press the case.

Nine alleged participants in mob actions were confined in the local jail. A *News Tribune* reporter who visited them found them confident, almost jovial. "Nine men were tramping up and down the corridor shouting 'Hup—hup,' of the army drillmaster, and majestically executing squads of right and left. They seemed to be enjoying confinement, or at least they were not morbidly pining away. Some laughed, some sang. Others marched through the drill with their hands on the shoulders of the man ahead, lifting their heels in the awkward goose-step of well regulated penitentiaries."

TRIAL *by* MOB

J*uly 10, 1920*—What bothered many Duluthians was that no positive identification had been made of any blacks. Neither had the blacks confessed nor given evidence against any other black. But some of the hostile reactions on the street, however, concluded that all of the blacks were guilty—if they hadn't committed the crime, they surely knew who did; because they refused to cooperate, they were at least guilty of obstructing justice. Many also believed the city would have been better off if the whole lot had been hanged back on June 15, saving the money for the trials.

Finally, Warren Greene struck upon a plan that brought some identifications. He ordered jailed blacks to be brought to the circus grounds that evening, where deputies and police were attempting to simulate conditions of the evening of June 14.

The weather approximated that June night, with temperatures tipping eighty degrees, and gentle westerly breezes swept a lilac ambrosia over much of West Duluth. It was an evening for gardening, and in the quiet residential neighborhoods, men in shirt-sleeves sprayed water over their lawns and rosebushes.

CIRCUS NEGROES TRIED ATTACK IN SOUTH BEND

SOUTH BEND, Ind., June 16.— Negroes employed by the same circus as those who were lynched in Duluth last night following an attack on a white girl, attempted to assault Helen Penrod of South Bend, when the show was in this city, June 7.

The assailants of the South Bend girl escaped, being hidden by companions, the police said here today.

from Virginia yesterday while the three men saved from the mob at police headquarters Tuesday night were brought from police headquarters.

Men Held.

The men being held at the county jail are: W. N. Miller, Louis Hays, Eugene Jefferson (Bluey), Frank Spider (Iron Jaw); Charles Harris (Fat Head); Earl Thomas (Hot Stuff); Albert Small (Blue); Nate Green (Fat); Loney Williams (Charley); Clarence Green, Norman Ousley (Tom); Max Mason (Brown Shirt) and John Thomas (Ouf).

Of the three men hung by the mob police officials say that only two made verbal confessions. Elmer Jackson and Eli Clayton are alleged to have admitted that they took part in alleged assault. The police say that Isaac McGhie, the third party hung, did not make any sort of a confession. He was the youngest of the trio and was taken out by the mob from the upper cells. McGhie was the first to be hung.

Farrell Saves Four.

Chief of Police John Murphy, Capt. Anthony Fiskett and Chief of Detectives Frank Schulte were returning to Duluth from Virginia with four of the negroes when they were met by Commissioner Bert Farrell and warned of the mob at police headquarters. The negroes were taken to Farrell's farm and left there in his charge while the police officials continued on their way to Duluth. It is believed by doing this they saved the lives of the four men.

MEN'S BLOCKADE TO FIUME.

FIUME, June 16.—A British tank

FATHER OF NEGR[O] DEPLORES LYN[CHING]

Girl Believes Dead Men [Right] Ones; Is Res[...]

That she was reasonably certain that the six negroes held at police headquarters Tuesday, three of which were hanged that night, were ones who had assaulted her was the statement yesterday by the girl victim of the men. She was at her home resting easily and is on the road to recovery.

"Their faces all looked alike to me as they were lined up for identification but from their voices and their build I'm sure they were some of the right ones," she said.

"For fear of committing a crime against an innocent person I hope there will be no more mob violence," her father said. "The courts and the law should be allowed to take their course. Undoubtedly the other guilty ones will be found out and brought to justice. I believe in doing as Father Powers urged the men to do Tuesday night.

"We want to thank the police and the circus officials in helping my daughter and the boy while they were identifying the men whom they thought committed the assault.

"I wanted to come down Tuesday night when I heard that a crowd was bent on action at the police station. I thought I might be able to get them to stop, but later felt that just my being there might incite them more so I didn't go down."

Speaking of the alleged assault, the girl said: "It wasn't much after 11 o'clock Monday night when it occurred. They were taking down the sideshow tent and the circus in the main tent was still on. For a few minutes we both watched them

"WHERE VAL[...]

There was a small crowd gathered at the nearby Athletic Park, where the Duluth Clydes baseball team hosted visiting Eveleth. Within earshot of the baseball game, thirteen blacks, in the clothes they wore on June 14, were standing on the old circus grounds at 9 PM.

Deputies then led Bobby Walsh and his father out to face the blacks. Max Mason, clad in a brown suit and cap, was told to step forward from the lineup and state his name. Then Greene asked him if he owned a pistol, and Mason replied, "No, sir!"

He was next ordered to back up a few steps, and he stood off about six feet. He was told to remove his cap, and then his coat, and finally was told to turn around before being ordered to face front. Greene hoped the sound of the blacks' voices might lead to identification, and he had instructed the young Walsh to try and remember how the blacks sounded, and to recall their general size and physique.

Greene then asked Mason how old he was. "Twenty-one years, sir," Mason said, his response coming in a slow, thick drawl that would be ridiculed in the Duluth papers.

"Max, where is your home town?"

"Lived in Decatur, Alabama."

"Any relatives?"

"Got a sister in Leighton, Alabama."

Greene looked at Walsh and the young man nodded, and quietly stated he thought Mason was the man with the gun. Greene was relieved at the breakthrough, and was further heartened when, ten minutes later, Walsh also identified William Miller as an accomplice.

The next evening at about the same time, Greene repeated the lineup in front of Sandra Teale, and once more Mason and Miller were identified. What was never clear, however, was whether or not Walsh and Miss Teale had the opportunity to discuss the men Walsh identified prior to Miss Teale's own attempt the following night.

Sandra recalled that the man with the gun was quite short,

and Mason, at five feet four inches, was the shortest of the blacks in police custody. He was not, however, the shortest black employed by the circus.

Armed with what he perceived as facts now, Greene was ready to begin trial preparations. But more than identification would be necessary—especially if that identification came nearly a month after the alleged assault.

A prevailing attitude among white northerners was that the Southern black was persecuted in Dixie with some justification. It was taken as a matter of course that the black was immoral. And Greene ordered all male black prisoners to undergo an examination for venereal disease. He also assigned Dr. William A. Coventry to examine Sandra Teale, who was found to have an advanced case of gonorrhea, probably contracted at least several months before the alleged assault.

On July 12, the jailed blacks were removed from their cells and individually brought before the grand jury. They were neither told they were being brought before the investigative body nor advised of their rights to refuse to testify. No attorney was present, and, indeed, none had been engaged to defend the prisoners.

In its benevolence, the grand jury informed the blacks that it simply wished to get at the truth. Those who had done nothing wrong had nothing to fear. Justice would be done, the blacks were told, but as long as prisoners continued to maintain silence in the face of overwhelming evidence, the truth could not quickly be determined. The implication was strong that, until the truth was revealed, the blacks would remain jailed.

During the late afternoon hours, the grand jury issued its findings, which did not deal at great length with the alleged assault. Instead, it found Murnian unfit for his job as Public Safety Commissioner. "His lack of action on June 15 has disgraced the police force and placed the foulest blot on the city ever known in its history," the report charged.

It also blasted Sgt. Olson. Despite his almost single-handed efforts to quell the mob, the report claimed his action or lack of it was open to severe criticism. The report summarized that the conduct of both men was most unbecoming, and the trust placed in them had been flagrantly violated.

The jury found that "No plan to handle the police or to repel an attack was decided upon beyond the use of water. Had the officer in charge issued rifles and bayonets and given the proper order, the mob would never have congregated and the Negroes would never have been murdered."

But the grand jury's work opened new criticisms. The *Duluth Labor World*, in its Saturday, June 16, editorial, claimed—"Thousands Support Murnian." The paper distributed to labor union members maintained that since the grand jury was comprised entirely of moneyed interests in the city, it based its attack on Murnian on political grounds. "There was not a shot heard," the weekly commented. "And if he had ordered police to shoot, these enemies would be after him with a vengeance."

The criticism of Sgt. Oscar Olson was particularly bitter to the officer who made forceful efforts to muster police to act within the restraint of Murnian's orders not to shoot. But Gen. Rhinow's investigation completely exonerated Olson, while seconding the condemnation of Murnian.

Rhinow's report revealed Duluth's police force numbered ninety-four persons, including officers, but only forth-nine were available for patrol duty, scattered over three shifts, at four stations throughout the city. And the report concluded:

Since Commissioner Murnian has served as Commissioner of Public Safety, he had taken no active steps toward inaugurating the proper discipline in the functioning of the police force.

Of all the ranking officers, only one, Sgt. Olson, was fully cognizant of the significance of his oath of office. He should be commended for having exercised an honest endeavor to perform his duty. Sgt. Olson made a valiant effort to disperse the mob in its early formation and prevent the lynching. Had his fellow officers been imbued with the proper instinct of discipline, the orders issued by Sgt. Olson would have unquestionably been carried out and the lynchings would doubtless have been avoided, notwithstanding the insufficient police force in Duluth.

It is the opinion of the undersigned that Com. Murnian erred appallingly in not requesting the assistance of the Sheriff or the state militia at a much earlier time than he did . . . He, having been present in the police station during the assembling of the mob, and the ultimate lynching, and not having exercised the duties required of him by his oath of office, is guilty of malfeasance in office. And has shown a woeful lack of courage, decision and competency.

While the General's report was not made public in Duluth, other criticisms of Murnian came from numerous civic groups. The commissioner, however, with assistance from *Labor World* editorials, weathered this crisis in his political life. He countered critics by arguing that if he had given orders to fire, the situation would have been worse. Duluthians agreed, and in April, 1921, he was returned to office by the voters.

Meanwhile, Chief Murphy had maintained a low profile, and had not spoken to Murnian. There was no question in his mind that he was being blamed by Murnian for the whole affair, and that Murnian would soon find a reason for suspension and dismissal.

That opportunity arose in mid-July, when Murphy was indicted for liquor smuggling. Though he would eventually be acquitted of the charge, his credibility suffered, and Murnian would refuse to reinstate him. Murphy sued, but the strain of the trial proved too great; he dropped the suit, and left the city.

On August 8, indictments were handed down against nineteen men on charges ranging from rioting to first-degree murder. All nineteen entered pleas of not guilty, and earned release by posting bond. Similarly, none of the blacks had been arraigned yet, and all remained in the county jail.

It was noteworthy, too, that all trials for indicted whites would occur long before blacks would be even formally charged. The first trial began on August 30 with Gilbert Henry Stephenson accused of rioting.

The courtroom was packed, and the city's mood was angry. One witness for the state lost his job and was evicted from his rented home because he had agreed to testify against Stephenson. He was called a traitor to his race, and endured much public loathing before Greene said he would investigate possible intimidation of the witnesses.

But the trial itself moved smoothly. Four boarders at the rooming house where Stephenson resided said that Hank was with them during the storming of the jail, though they all had observed the attack. Under cross-examination, however, all admitted they were not with Stephenson during the entire evening.

Most damaging evidence came from Nate Natelson, himself a defendant, who agreed to turn state's evidence, and identified Stephenson as a rioter.

On September 2, after six hours of deliberation, Stephenson was convicted and sentenced to not more than five years in prison.

William Rozon's trial also began on the 30th, but it ended in a hung jury. Despite testimony from Lt. Barber and Jacob Nystrom identifying Rozon as a participant, the jury found itself hopelessly deadlocked after deliberating thirty-two hours.

On September 13, Louis Dondino was convicted when the jury rejected the defense argument that although Dondino was driving the green truck, he was unaware that his passengers were bent on rioting. He was convicted of inciting to riot, and like Stephenson, received five years.

The following day, John Burr, who was startled by his arrest in June, was acquitted in less than two hours after several people testified about his law and order activity. Forceful testimony in his behalf came from Loney Williams who told the court that Burr had saved his life when the crowd demanded the men in the cell to "Give us boots."

Also on September 13, nineteen-year-old Carl Hammerberg was convicted of rioting. Then Pat Olson was acquitted, and the sting seemed to go out of the trials of mob leaders. In the city, people voiced concern that some should be convicted while others, some of whose roles had been more prominent, went free.

Included in this group was Leonard Hedman who was acquitted after lengthy jury deliberation. Acting as his own witness, Hedman told the court that his remarks were misinterpreted by police, and, in fact, he made only neutral comments during the riot. Since his alleged role was one of the most active among mob members, acquittal signalled the end of trials for those arrested, and all murder charges were dropped.

Duluthians found themselves uneasy about convicting men who carried out their own sympathies, and felt the issue would best be forgotten. And in homes in West Duluth, talk regarding the lynchings stopped, although adults occasionally whispered about justice being upset when black rapists would get a simple jail sentence for a crime worse than murder.

The stage was set for trials of Max Mason and William Miller.

Hostility surfaced anew and security around the blacks remained tight. The mood in Duluth was mixed, of agitation and anxiety, coupled with relief that finally the blacks would be punished by law. But among the city's blacks, the feeling was that the original crime was a frame-up, a fraud, and bitterness mounted. Justice, they believed, was for whites only. Three black men were brutally slain, and no one was punished for the killings.

TRIAL *by* MOB

Max Mason was a native of Decatur, Alabama, where he grew up the younger of two children born to sharecropper parents. His formal schooling consisted of one week in the first grade. Most of his early childhood was spent foraging for food or looking for odd jobs. He worked somewhat steadily on cotton plantations as a picker until his mother died in 1916.

Later that year he obtained a job in a local hotel kitchen, remaining there until the death of his father in 1917. He then left Alabama for Louisville, Kentucky, and found employment as a hotel dishwasher. Through acquaintances in the hotel kitchen, he heard about the circus. The circus, he was told, offered decent jobs to black folks, and the treatment was better than in cotton fields or hot kitchens. The circus provided meals and a bed and a chance to travel all over the country.

The young man must have thought it would be nice to get around, see how things were up north, where he was told a colored man didn't have to tip his hat to white men on the streets. And there wouldn't be much chance in getting lonesome either. Most all the crews were black, and the work was fine. If you kept your nose clean, he was told, they'd take you on again next year, too. And if you only had gone to school one week out of your life, had no family, and yearned to travel, hitching on with the circus seemed just the thing to do.

Mason joined the Robinson show on April 24, 1920, in Peru, Indiana, and worked in the cook house during the day and in the Big Top at night. He liked circus life, and saw that it might be all right to stay with. When the blacks got older, if they'd kept a good record, they mostly waited tables, cooked or tidied up about the kitchen. Certainly a future with the circus looked promising to young Max Mason.

He had been warned that Northern cops could be rough on blacks, and if he was caught with a bottle of hootch, he could expect a few knots on the head as well as a stretch in jail. So, after his arrest in Virginia, Minnesota, he did not find his subsequent treatment out of the ordinary.

But discussions with cellmates during his imprisonment did little to bolster his spirits. The jury would accept as absolute fact that a frail white girl was raped by "niggers." After all, why would she lie about such an ordeal—no matter what the "niggers" said, the whites reasoned.

Because the blacks refused to open up before the grand jury in July, they were told not to expect any leniency. Mason's only hope was that his lawyers—Ferdinand Lee Barnett, Jr., from Chicago, and R.C. McCullouch, from St. Paul—could prove that the girl lied about the rape.

The attorneys representing blacks were themselves black men, hired by the St. Paul NAACP for $1200. It was thought in some circles that the men would have been wiser to select white lawyers instead of "nigger lawyers" as they were often called in Duluth. But most white attorneys in Duluth believed the men were guilty, and probably did not wish to jeopardize their standings in the community by representing blacks accused of raping a white girl. Those consulted did say that the blacks would be better off pleading guilty and throwing themselves on the mercy of the court. The only lawyers willing to gamble with the "not guilty" pleas were the blacks hired by the NAACP.

A third attorney, Charles Scrutchin, from Bemidji, Minnesota, had been retained to defend Miller. And of the three lawyers, Barnett carried the most impressive credentials. He was the oldest son of F.L. Barnett, Sr., founder of the *Conservator*, the first black newspaper in Chicago. His stepmother was noted Negro rights activist Ida Wells. Barnett had served as an assistant county attorney for Cook County and earned respect in legal circles. Mason was repeatedly assured how fortunate he was to have a lawyer of Mr. Barnett's reputation.

While Warren Greene had all along hoped for confessions that would clear the air, they did not develop, and there were many Duluthians who believed that it was the black lawyers who confused the men and kept them from confessing. If the blacks listened to the smart-aleck lawyers, they would be sorry for it, felt many white citizens.

Still, Greene had reason for suspicion, too. He may have thought that the stories of Walsh and Miss Teale lacked credibility and might be cracked by an aggressive defense which in turn could free the blacks. And that would all but seal Green's fate as far as his being able to capture a seat on the district court bench. He determined to press hard for convictions, just as he had struggled to convict whites from the mob. However, his handling of both the whites and blacks made him an anathema to St. Louis County voters who overwhelmingly rejected him in the November balloting. Magney, whom Greene had easily outdistanced in the April primary, defeated Greene by over five thousand votes.

After Dr. Coventry's examination in July had revealed Sandra Teale's infection, Greene had ordered all blacks examined, and Dr. M.A. Nicholson of Duluth was assigned to carry out Greene's edict.

Edgy from confinement, irritated because they had not been formally charged with any crime, several of the prisoners balked at the doctor's request that they submit to tests for venereal disease. Nicholson tried to reassure them by saying if they were clean they had nothing to worry about. But it was a jailer who sneered, "If you don't cooperate, we'll toss you in the dungeon and put you on bread and water," that intimidated the prisoners into cooperation.

Though no evidence of collusion exists in this matter, the circumstances surrounding the examination and the report from Dr. Nicholson that Max Mason also had an advanced case of the disease became highly suspect. Mason himself protested vigorously that he did not have a "dose," although he did admit contracting gonorrhea over a year earlier in Louisville. But, he insisted, he had been cured. He would maintain this throughout his trial. The medical report, however, said that Mason was infected.

Probably based on this evidence, it was decided that Mason would be tried first. One juror, a prominent banker, seriously considered approaching Mason and telling him that he would use his influence to arrange a short sentence if Mason would only cooperate. He believed that he might even help Mason find a job, upon his release from prison.

The talk circulating around Duluth at that time was that no jury could acquit a man who had to get those outside "nigger lawyers" to defend himself; they were only asking for trouble.

Then, as now, in Duluth, November is the cruelest month. Bitter northeast winds whip the city from off the lake, and bring a premature frigidity. The city's trees, long since bare of foliage, stand like gaunt, bony ghosts of a distant summer past, and fragile, dry leaves swirl along gutters rustling with grit and coal dust. It was long-underwear weather now; it bespoke chapped hands and cracked, bleeding lips. There was not enough snow for children's sliding, but enough to serve as a forewarning of the violent gusts of white and ice which would soon threaten to paralyze the town.

November in Duluth is an omnipresent gray. The temper of the city in 1920 was edgy, nervous. Fall was forgotten. Pray God would keep winter tolerable. But get November over with.

November 8, 1920—A sudden and raging storm hit Duluth with winds of thirty-six miles an hour. Rain turned to sleet, then snow. By morning of the ninth, the temperature had plunged to zero, and six inches of white blanketed the city. Under more normal conditions, the storm might have been something to talk about with folks back in Alabama. But Max Mason was awaiting trial, which was now set for November 22. In the meantime, he had been in jail for five months and twelve days, and no doctor had been sent to treat his "advanced case of gonorrhea."

November 22 broke dry and cold. The state of Minnesota vs. Max Mason. Judge W.A. Cant presiding.

The young Mason must have been bewildered by the austere atmosphere of the court room, but he took some solace from his lawyers. Convinced of his own innocence, he placed great trust in these men. They were men of education, who happened to be black—and who else was there to trust?

But his defense would prove woefully inept. Communication between the Twin Cities' chapter of the NAACP—which hired both the Employer's Detective Service and the attorneys—was sadly lacking. There is no evidence suggesting that any of the attorneys saw Morgan's report which pointed to inconsistencies between statements Sandra Teale gave police and statements she gave him. Neither was there any indication that attorneys knew that Dr. Graham said he didn't believe the girl had been raped.

Further, it was apparent from the beginning that both Mason's lawyers sought to mollify the white jurors by not appearing overly aggressive or insulting. They did not even insinuate that Sandra Teale may have been lying. They based the defense on the premise that while the girl had probably been assaulted, Max Mason had not been a participant.

Still, the case for Mason seemed to go well at first. Barnett managed to bring out discrepancies in the testimonies of police officers who were asked to identify Mason in court. One thought Mason was one of the four men brought down from Virginia by Chief Murphy, while another believed he was one of the original six held in jail. Both were wrong, Barnett pointed out. Mason came down on the train from Virginia the following day. Also, Barnett argued, Mason wasn't even identified until nearly a month after the alleged attack took place.

Sandra Teale and Robert Walsh both took the stand and gave accounts of what happened the night of June 14. But neither was rigidly cross-examined. Defense lawyers simply requested restatements of their testimonies, and throughout appeared to handle the two with a distant gentility, not willing to probe and dig, not willing—or perhaps not able—to go the full distance in an effort to secure a victory for their client.

McCullouch and Barnett were, perhaps, feeling out a sensitive jury—a jury that surely believed beyond a doubt that the girl had been assaulted. Perhaps the jury might have thought the rape did not happen precisely as stated by the witnesses, but it did take place. It must have. Why else would there have been all this furor and the horror of the lynchings?

Dr. Graham was also called as a state witness, but was not especially helpful. His statement was not as forthright as it was when he spoke to Morgan. "Evidence of assault was inconclusive," he said. "I cannot say for sure whether or not she was raped."

Incredibly, the defense did not press Graham for clarification, or elaboration, but allowed the statement to stand. Then, prosecutor Greene called Dr. Coventry who related finding Miss Teale infected with gonorrhea. The girl, who said she first noticed the infection ten days to two weeks after the assault of June 14, later told the court she noticed the infection about three days before the doctor came to examine her on July 14. Dr. Coventry, under cross-examination, said the infection should have followed in one to ten days after contact.

Cross-examining Sandra Teale, McCullouch asked, "Did you tell your mother about the infection?"

"No," she replied.

McCullouch emphasized that Miss Teale did not contact a physician on her own; she was examined by Dr. Coventry at the request of the prosecuting attorney.

The state, weakened slightly, called Dr. Nicholson for the trump card. The doctor told the jury that in his examination of all prisoners, only Mason was found to be infected with gonorrhea. And this was precisely what the jurors had waited for. One juror later admitted, "It was the gonorrhea thing that clinched it." Other testimony from Sandra and Bobby might have been all loose ends, but here was concrete proof—proof the jury could use to vote a conviction, and assuage any twinges of conscience that might otherwise have lingered.

Finally, Mason testified in his own behalf, taking exception to Dr. Nicholson. "I don't have no gonorrhea," he said, claiming that if the girl had been raped, he had nothing to do with it. He said he was actively loading empty seats into boxcars at the time of the alleged assault. His story was corroborated by Loney Williams, but the damage had been done. The expert testimony of a literate white man more than offset the denial of that evidence by an illiterate black man.

Friday, November 26, 1920—In his closing argument, Warren Greene told the jury that this case was the most important he'd ever brought into court. "Why do we have mobs?" he asked. "It is because people think the Negroes won't be convicted. That's why they take the law into their own hands. People of Duluth and St. Louis County want to know through your verdict that when a white girl is ravished by a black or white man and the man is proven guilty, as in this case, the man is going to be found guilty."

Barnett, summing up for the defense, argued that the state had wholly failed to present its case against Mason. He scored Walsh for the attitude he claimed to have taken. "Anglo-Saxon blood never permits attacks upon its women without a protest. Something might have happened on the circus grounds that night. Perhaps the girl's ring might have been taken or stolen, or the boy's watch taken, but the offense charted in this indictment was not committed by this defendant."

Barnett drew an angry reaction from Greene by insinuating that he had schooled witnesses for the prosecution by having Walsh and Miss Teale identify defendants by physical shape and stride. "Is it fair to send a man to the penitentiary on that identification? I don't ask any favors for a black man—only justice. The law says that nobody shall be convicted on his own evidence. The law has been shamefully abused in this case. The men were compelled to testify against themselves before the Grand Jury without being warned."

It was late Friday night when the jury received the instructions from Judge Cant, but the jurors were allowed to go home for the night and begin deliberations in the morning.

9:51 AM, Saturday, November 27, 1920—Jury discussion began with an air of uneasiness. True, Walsh had been examined by Dr. Coventry as well, and he was found to be clean. Still, rumors persisted concerning the character of the boy, and the girl, too, for that matter. But whatever, the girl had suffered enough already . . .

3:25 PM—The jury returned a guilty verdict, and Duluthians heaved a collective sigh of relief. At last the nasty business was over. The proof was in: the blacks had raped the girl.

Monday, November 29, 1920—Mason, facing Judge Cant for sentencing, insisted once more that he was not diseased and asked to be examined by a court-appointed physician. He pointed out that he had not been treated by a doctor during the more than five months since his arrest, except when he was checked after complaining of a cold. And again he repeated, "I didn't do it. I'm not guilty."

His request for an impartial physical examination was denied, and he was sentenced to thirty years at the state prison at Stillwater.

TRIAL *by* MOB

*uesday, November 30, 1920*—The State of Minnesota vs. William Miller. Judge William Cant, presiding.

Most Duluthians had been satisfied by Mason's conviction. The girl had been raped, and at least one man would go to prison. There was little furor over Miller's trial, consequently, and the courtroom was comparatively spare of spectators.

Little is known about Miller except that he lived in Cincinnati, Ohio, with his sister. It was obvious that Mason's conviction upset Miller, and when he appeared in court, he looked weak and drawn, a sharp contrast to the man defending him. Charles Scrutchin was notably relaxed, almost arrogant. He had been deeply bothered by the inept defense of Max Mason, and gauging the attitude of the jurors, Scrutchin believed Mason could have earned acquittal. What was lacking there was a vigorous, forceful attack on the testimonies of state witnesses, especially Sandra Teale. Scrutchin also believed that Mason's lawyers did not press the case along racial lines. Would the jury be so quick to convict a white man for assaulting a black girl?

At the same time, Scrutchin knew he must proceed with a certain degree of caution. Yet, caution was not one of Charlie Scrutchin's prominent traits. He was married to a white woman, and practiced law in Bemidji, Minnesota. At the time of his arrival in that city, in 1904, there was only one other black family in residence. Because of his mixed marriage, Scrutchin would have little social life in the community during his years of practice there. If prejudice existed in Bemidji, however, it was often overlooked by persons seeking legal assistance, and Scrutchin developed a successful practice among working people in Bemidji. Folks there frequently allowed that "the colored lawyer is one smart man."

Possessing a quick and nimble mind, he was frequently labeled brilliant by peers. A white man with his credentials would have undoubtedly gone far in legal circles at that time. However, Scrutchin was not a great favorite among some Minnesota blacks. He had built something of a reputation defending whites who were taken to court for grievances by blacks. The concept of a black lawyer defending a white man against another black man made profound impressions on white juries, and no doubt earned Scrutchin tidy fees, as he won case after case.

Scrutchin must have known what his reputation was among some area blacks. Few, however, could dispute his legal skills. And when push came to shove, Scrutchin was first of all a black who had also felt the sting of prejudice and racial abuse. He was proud to offer his services to the NAACP in a case representing such a gross miscarriage of justice.

He had probably angered Barnett, chiding him for his kid gloves approach to Mason's jury and state witnesses. It was a tragic mistake, he noted, and would not be repeated in Miller's trial. If he were to lose this, he would lose fighting. And Charlie Scrutchin was a tough, relentless in-fighter. He would not be easily defeated.

Scrutchin openly doubted that the rape took place at all, and on Tuesday during his cross-examination of Dr. Graham, he made certain the jury was aware of that. "Assuming the girl's story is true, and that she had fainted at the time the assault took place, would not an attack by six Negroes upon the girl have left physical evidence of tears or lacerations?" he asked.

Graham responded, "I do not think I would have found her in a normal condition the next morning."

Attempting to blunt this damaging testimony, Greene called in Drs. S.H. Boyer and A.K. McDonald. Both testified that it would have been possible for the assault to have occurred without noticeable evidence. But Scrutchin continued the attack, forcing the doctors to admit they had no first hand knowledge of any similar case. His voice rising, he asked Dr. Boyer, "You have never had any experience embracing all these elements, have you, Doctor?"

"No," said Dr. Boyer.

Both sides concluded arguments on Tuesday. Greene, sensing the weakness in his case, made an emotional, impassioned summation for the state—"Testimony in this case is undisputed that she was a virgin. God knows she has suffered enough already without having a jury say to her that she is not only a liar, but that she contracted the disease communicated to her by Mason from some other person. What are you going to say to her with your verdict? Are you going to brand her as a falsifier and a prostitute?"

Scrutchin calmly asked the jury to lay aside natural prejudice of a white man against a black man. "If this boy on trial was a white boy, and the complaining witness a colored girl, there would be no occasion for me to argue this case before you. Prejudice? Certainly there is prejudice. We know there is prejudice. This defendant knows that his race is hated, and that his color is a crime. No matter how fair you gentlemen of the jury may be, if you return a verdict of guilty there will always be a lingering suspicion in his mind that he was not given a fair chance because he was black . . . Still, I believe that you are going to be fair in this case. That there is still a little spark of justice burning, and you will give this boy the presumption of innocence the law says is his."

Deliberately, Scrutchin approached the jury box and stared at the members. "If this girl was ravished as she claims to have been ravished, she would have been taken to a morgue instead of her home."

Thursday, December 2, was sunny and cold. Downtown merchants were thinking the bright weather would start the annual trek of Christmas shoppers into the stores. Superior Street traffic was punctuated by the tinkling bells of Salvation Army ringers. And in his cell, William Miller wept and told Scrutchin he wanted to go home for Christmas. He would get his wish. After a six-hour deliberation, the jury found Miller not guilty.

The jubilant young man embraced Scrutchin and told reporters, "I'm going back to Cincinnati where my sister keeps house for me. I've got about two hundred dollars back pay coming from the circus."

With this acquittal, Judge Cant dismissed charges against five other blacks, and Greene abandoned prosecution of the rest. Strongest evidence pointed toward Mason and Miller, while evidence against the other men was largely speculative.

Meanwhile, Max Mason, increasingly aware that his conviction rested entirely on Dr. Nicholson's testimony, looked more hopefully toward the appeal which might free him—especially since Miller's acquittal. He continued his claim that he was free of gonorrhea, and had not been treated for the disease since his June 15 arrest. But his appeal was denied.

Friday, December 10, 1920—The infamy was ended, and many were trying to forget it ever happened. There was the Christmas season to look forward to now, and the kids would be out of school in a week or so. There was enough snow for the season, and the city was pretty at night with the sprinkling of Christmas lights lining Superior Street.

West End and West Duluth residents of Italian, Serbian, and Slavik descents tested the wines made for the holidays. Prohibition or not, a man could drink some wine with his friends, and there wasn't anything the law could do about it. Across the frozen St. Louis River bay in Superior, certain men from Duluth sat in small speakeasies, their day's labor completed at the steel plant or the railroad. They would pour down a slug of Canadian whiskey and look past each other, their eyes red from wind and whiskey. Their laughter would be strained and forced. The normally jovial greeting of "Merry Christmas" to their fellows sounded somehow empty and hollow.

And such men would acknowledge each other with furtive nods, meaningless claps on the back. They felt in their guts that what they did was right, but they still needed to exorcise the shreds of guilt. Occasionally, someone might have muttered that it would be a long time before "niggers" tried anything with white women in Minnesota again.

Except for this small knot of hardliners, there was little talk of the lynchings. Duluth was a city ashamed. It wanted to forget.

Christmas Eve, 1920—Max Mason was still in the Duluth jail. Down the hall, some prisoners were eating their evening meal. Mason was not hungry. He had no visitors. Neither did he have gonorrhea

Mob.

dequate to
on. Says
l.

Not to Use
Many
ury.

LIVES ARE CHOKED OUT

WHERE HANGING TOOK PLACE

IN

EPILOGUE

January 11, 1921—Max Mason was brought to Stillwater State Prison, two weeks before Dondino and Stephenson were committed to the institution, having exhausted their appeals. Hammerberg was sent to the state reformatory at St. Cloud.

November 1922—Mason's case was appealed to the Minnesota Supreme Court, but the conviction was sustained. One argument in support of the conviction noted that it was common knowledge that among Northern whites the identification of Southern blacks was difficult. But the fact that Mason was identified by both Robert Walsh and Sandra Teale gave credence to the conviction.

Justice Homer B. Dibbel, filing the minority opinion, referred to Dr. Graham's examination of the girl, which concluded a normal condition was present. Dibbel wrote, "There was perhaps a possibility that six Negroes committed the crime just as charged. Convictions are not rested on possibilities. The story in its entirety is unusual and strikingly improbable." Noting the conviction largely was based on the gonorrhea issue, Dibbel stated that to convict Mason on that evidence was to imply that every infected male in Duluth, white or black, the night of June 15, 1920, was also guilty of the rape.

March 1923—Louis Dondino and Henry Stephenson were paroled, two years and two months after entering prison.

February 1925—In an almost unprecedented move, the parole board released Mason. Rape conviction meant a minimum of twelve years in Minnesota. Mason served only four. And blacks convicted of assaulting whites could be expected to serve nearly a full thirty-year sentence. The mysterious and unusual action of the Board may never be determined. All records concerning this case have been destroyed. And in Duluth, itself, few files are maintained on the lynchings. The St. Louis County Historical Society, in an attempt to discourage research into the unseemly, carries virtually no information at all on the episode.

Yet, other mysteries remain. Among Duluth blacks with a strong oral history tradition, it is reported that at least three of the white men involved in mob activities themselves met with violent and unsolved deaths. One report states that two bodies were recovered in a refrigerator railroad car about two years after the lynchings, while a third body was found in a roadside ditch. While older blacks insist these stories are true, apparently no on remembers the names of the victims, nor where the bodies were found. This aspect then must remain speculative, for records in St. Louis County through 1925 do not indicate unnatural deaths for any of those involved with the mob.

Meanwhile, according to many Duluth blacks, the housing restrictions which had previously been unspoken and somewhat inconsistent, became absolute. It became difficult for Duluth blacks to obtain homes in traditional residential areas until the 1960s.

The situation in education also became critical. Though black students were allowed to enroll at Duluth State Teachers College, they were not allowed to practice teach in the Duluth public schools. Since this preparation was mandated by the state, the effect of this unwritten prohibition was to deny black teachers the opportunity to become certified teachers in Duluth.

At the time of the lynching in the city, about eighteen employees in the U.S. Post Office were blacks of longstanding tenure. According to a former NAACP president in Duluth, no new black workers were hired by the local postal service until the 1960s.

Among the principals involved in this story, Sandra Teale married and lived in Superior, Wisconsin, never to discuss any aspect of this case with reporters.

Robert Walsh, too, attempted to find himself in the normal

mainstream of life in Duluth. However, those who knew him observed a marked personality change after the lynchings. A priest who knew him described him as almost quiet, retiring. A man who remembered playing basketball against him said the old flamboyance was gone in later years, and that he lost the self-assuredness that marked his teenage years.

After his re-election to office in 1921, Public Safety Commissioner William Murnian saw the lynching incident surface again in 1923 when he sought his third term. Duluthians apparently had reflected on the tragedy and wished the incident could be forgotten. Murnian was the last vestige of that horror, and though other commissioners strongly urged his reelection, he was soundly defeated in April 1923, and never returned to public office in the city.

Sgt. Oscar Olson, who absorbed considerable heat locally in the aftermath of the lynchings but who had bravely upheld his oath of office, stayed on to become chief of police which, for years in Duluth, was a position appointed by the mayor and the commissioners. When a new mayor was elected in 1938, Olson became chief of detectives. In 1941, while attempting to make an arrest, he was shot and killed by the suspect.

Police officers Fiskett and Barber continued on the force and so did sons of the men. Other officers still enjoyed community support and remained with the force also. Duluthians believed that since the hands of policemen were tied, they could not be held accountable for the lynchings.

Eddie Nichols remained in Duluth for about thirty years after the lynchings, and helped the city overcome racial prejudices. A founder and officer of the local NAACP, Nichols operated his own catering business in the city until retiring to reside in St. Paul.

W.F. Rodney, who owned the home in which Nichols lived at the time of the lynching, would later have an ironic brush with attorney

Charles Scrutchin. Scrutchin, who returned to private practice in Bemidji, continued his practice of representing white clients in cases against blacks. Rodney, who was seeking a grievance against a white, saw the skillful Scrutchin win for the defendant.

Warren E. Greene, the prosecuting attorney who lost his bid for a seat on the district bench, left Duluth in 1928 because of declining health. He died in Washington, Connecticut, in June 1937.

Of all the men involved in mob activity, the most noted was Leonard Hedman. At the time of the arrest and trial, he was supposedly planning to attend law school. This ambition was not realized, however, and Hedman left Duluth to become a resort owner and operator.

Other principals in the mob, as far as can be determined, experienced genuine shame at the happening, and many went on to lead exemplary lives, becoming involved with various civic and youth programs throughout the city. None would discuss the lynchings again, and to this day descendants express surprise that their relatives ever were involved in the tragedy.

Fred W. Beecher, the National Guard officer who figured significantly in mopping-up operations, remained in the Guard until 1929. However, his work during the lynching incident was of no consequence in his military career, and at the time of his discharge he was still a major.

J.A.A. Burnquist, governor of the state, spent the next nineteen years in private law practice before returning to public life. In 1939, he was elected state attorney general and served in that post until 1955.

The final ignominy was the location of the burial sites of Isaac McGhie, Elmer Jackson and Elias Clayton. For more than 70 years following the lynching, it was believed the three laid in unmarked graves in a potters' field near the Duluth Cook home, a residence for the indigent. However, the bodies of the victims had been taken to Park Hill Cemetary, owned at the time by a local Lutheran church. The graves of the men remained unmarked until 1991. The rationale for not designating those burial sites seems clear. To have done so in June 1920 would possibly have led to desecration of the graves. Feeling about the lynching and its aftermath ran high in the city for many years. Perhaps city fathers believed that secret burial in unmarked plots would prevent acts of vandalism. And, given the temper of those unfortunate times, perhaps such a rationale is not to be faulted.

Today, however, the bodies of the three men — no longer forgotten — rest in commemorated graves. Just three miles from the streetcorner where that enraged mob exacted its twisted justice, new markers honor the memory of Isaac McGhie, Elmer Jackson and Elias Clayton.

Michael Fedo, a Duluth native, is the author of five books, including *One Shining Season* and *Chronicles of Aunt Hilma.* His most recent book is *The Man from Lake Wobegon.*

The publisher wishes to thank the following for their cooperation in realizing this book:

Bob Baldwin

Susan Christensen

Gary Doty

Bob Jodon and *The Duluth News Tribune*

Jerry Hallberg, Rick Kollath, and Brigid Pajunen
of Kollath Graphic Design

Geraldine Richelson

The St. Louis County Historical Society

The Minnesota Historical Society

Steven Senenfelder of Custom Photo-Lab

Johanna Tani

Susan Walker

Claudie Washington
and the Duluth chapter of the NAACP

David Ouse and the reference staff
of the Duluth Public Library